IMAGES
of Rail

RAILROADS OF LOS GATOS

Billy Jones (1884–1968) is a name synonymous with the railroad in Los Gatos. A railroader for his entire professional career, Jones was among the finest engineers to serve the Southern Pacific. He retired in 1949 after nearly six decades on the Coast Division. Jones is best known for his "Wildcat Railroad," the 1/3-scale, 18-inch gauge live steam railway he built and operated at his Daves Avenue prune orchard for the enjoyment of neighborhood children. (Courtesy Barbara Phinney; BJWRR collection.)

ON THE COVER: A regular on the San Francisco–Los Gatos commute in the 1950s, Engine No. 2476 backs toward town with a railfan special on April 25, 1954. While the arrival and destination were the same, this trip detoured through Niles and San Jose via the Dumbarton Rail Bridge. (Photograph by Charlie Givens; courtesy Eddie Chase.)

IMAGES
of Rail

RAILROADS OF
LOS GATOS

Edward Kelley with Peggy Conaway

ARCADIA
PUBLISHING

Published by Arcadia Publishing
Charleston, South Carolina

Library of Congress Catalog Card Number: 2006924922

For all general information contact Arcadia Publishing at:
Telephone 843-853-2070
Fax 843-853-0044
E-mail sales@arcadiapublishing.com
For customer service and orders:
Toll-Free 1-888-313-2665

Visit us on the Internet at www.arcadiapublishing.com

For Donna M. Plehn (1936–2002).
A teacher and friend who shared her love of
California history with many—E. K.

CONTENTS

ACKNOWLEDGMENTS

What lies before you is a collaborative effort of historians, collectors, railroaders, railroad enthusiasts, librarians, and longtime residents of our town to document the colorful but often forgotten railroading history in the "Gem City of the Foothills." Whether sharing their time, photographs, scanning skills, or tales of the rails, there are many to be thanked.

In no particular order, I thank Geraldine Peters, Betty Ermert, Phil Reader, Tom Shreve, Jim Holmes, Eddie Chase, Barbara Phinney, Charlie Hopkins, Ken Middlebrook, Chuck Bergtold, Paul Kopach, Dick Sparrer at the *Los Gatos Weekly-Times*, Barbara Baggerly, Peter Panacy, Dave Adams, Tom Mongouvan, Jack Vodden, Elayne Shore Shuman, Mary Gillespie-Greenberg, Lyn Dougherty, and Dudley Warner.

Thank you all.

INTRODUCTION

While the rails may be gone and the depot long since demolished, Los Gatos remains very much a railroad town. In 1877, a year before regular service began, a wood-fired, cinder-belching steam locomotive arrived in town on rails just three feet wide. The advent of the Iron Horse would play a prominent role in defining the economy and culture of Los Gatos. A ceremonious pulling-of-a-spike in 1959 ended more than 80 years of the "big railroad," yet the railroading spirit continues to linger here, largely thanks to a celebrated engineer whose legacy has enabled the steam locomotive to survive for future generations.

The earliest settlers of Los Gatos brought with them dreams of claiming their fortune in gold. Mostly farmers, they found Los Gatos's Mediterranean climate ideal, settling in this natural gateway between the fertile Santa Clara Valley and the towering Santa Cruz Mountains. While gold was not to be found in these hills, settlers would realize the value of another natural resource—virgin stands of towering Coast Redwoods. By the 1860s, about a dozen sawmills had sprouted in the hills south of Los Gatos with milling boards and beams for shipments to the mines of New Almaden, the Mother Lode, and beyond.

In 1854, Scottish immigrant James Alexander Forbes believed a flour mill along Los Gatos Creek would be a lucrative venture. As most of the flour in the area was then imported from South America, the mill would provide both a local source and means of production. A combination of poor management and inadequate headwater brought Forbes to bankruptcy just three years later, but the mill would finally become successful after 1870, when it became the Los Gatos Manufacturing Company.

Prior to 1880, a trip over the Santa Cruz Mountains by horse or stage was a hazardous and uncomfortable affair. A four-hour journey from San Jose, combined with the threats of grizzly bears, bandits, and nefarious toll keepers, left passengers and merchants begging for a more practical alternative.

In a San Francisco saloon, Comstock millionaire James "Slippery Jim" Fair mapped out a rail line for banker Alfred "Hog" Davis, one that would connect the city with the shores of Monterey Bay at Santa Cruz. Sequestered by tree-shrouded mountains, Santa Cruz, a sprawling industrial center, was an untapped market that the Southern Pacific was most anxious to claim. The city's bustling seaport was the third busiest in California at the time, with lumber mills, tanneries, and the California Powder Works located nearby. In a daring attempt to undermine the Southern Pacific, Fair and Davis purchased the assets of a failed start-up line, the Santa Clara Valley Railroad, and in 1876, the audacious duo founded the South Pacific Coast Railroad.

At the 1876 Centennial Exposition in Philadelphia, James Fair learned of the extensive network of narrow-gauge lines being built by the Denver and Rio Grande Railroad in the Colorado Rockies. With rails three feet apart and lighter equipment, narrow-gauge railroads had a specific advantage over rough terrain, accommodating tighter turning radii with greatly reduced construction costs. Rather than the conventional four-foot, eight-and-a-half-inch standard gauge, Fair, largely influenced by representatives of the Baldwin Locomotive Works, decided to build his line as a narrow-gauge road. Construction began later in 1876 at Dumbarton Point in the East Bay, extending south towards Santa Clara and San Jose. Resting on gravel ballast extracted from the banks of Los Gatos Creek, the tracks reached Campbell and the edge of Los Gatos in 1877 when construction came to a halt as surveyors contemplated the remainder of the route. One option would bring the line through Boulder Creek via Saratoga, while another proposed running through Mountain Charley Gulch to Soquel. Objections by Santa Cruz entrepreneur Fred Hihn, who feared rival development in neighboring Soquel, contributed to the decision to travel through Los Gatos Creek Canyon towards Felton. From there, the remainder of the line would roughly follow a right-of-way completed by the Santa Cruz and Felton Railroad in 1875.

Despite the terrain it traversed, the mountain line was a surprisingly tame railroad. While initial surveys proposed switchbacks and grades of three percent or more, Fair, who had extensive mining experience, was determined to keep travel times as short as possible and called in his engineers from the Comstock Lode to bore more than three miles of tunnels through the Santa Cruz Mountains. They kept curves relatively tame and the grades less than two percent, climbing a summit less than 1,000 feet above sea level. The same could not be said for the more tortuous Santa Cruz and Felton portion of the line, though a small tunnel and other work still made the winding line viable.

By the end of 1877, the railroad was built through Los Gatos and construction was well on its way through Cats' Canyon. The site chosen for a depot at Los Gatos was the location of John Lyndon's Ten Mile House, the town's earliest hostelry. An exchange of $50 allowed the hotel to be moved across the street and the site made available for a depot and freight shed. With Los Gatos as its southern terminus, passenger service, via a ferry connection at Newark, was inaugurated to San Francisco that year. A single-stall enginehouse and turntable, located at Elm Street and Boone Lane, were particularly useful during the days when Los Gatos was the end of the line, a title it reclaimed in 1940.

The arduous task of laying track over "the hill" was accomplished almost entirely by Chinese laborers, 600 of whom were enlisted by the Ning Yeung Company of San Francisco. For their meager pay, these men risked their lives to cut, clear, bore, and blast the rails through the mountains. When the job was done, more than 60 had died, many in the frequent gas-pocket explosions that occurred during construction of the line's tunnels. Cornish "Gandy Dancers" performed much of the later tunnel labor after the superstitious Chinese crews, believing the tunnels were cursed, refused to work on them. After the monumental task was completed in 1880, many Chinese workers remained in residency behind the rail yards and along Los Gatos Creek, though they suffered the effects of the town's strong anti-Chinese sentiments.

With the route opened to Santa Cruz, the ferry terminal moved from Newark to Alameda. The trip from San Francisco to Santa Cruz could be now accomplished in a little over three hours, impressive for the time. Additional branchlines were later built to tap lumber resources in Boulder Creek and the quicksilver mines of New Almaden.

The scenery on the Santa Cruz Mountain line was breathtaking, and lengthy "picnic trains" ran on weekends to serve the mountain resorts of Glenwood, Laurel, Mount Hermon, and Sunset Park, established by the Southern Pacific in the 1890s. Sacks of wheat flour soon gave way to carloads of fruit, which were hauled from the orchards to the canneries across Santa Clara Valley. Canned fruit loaded on the Los Gatos Canning Company spur across Santa Cruz Avenue was shipped to points as far away as New York City and Liverpool, England.

Los Gatos became an important rest stop where locomotives took on water before starting up "the hill." In 1887, with Jim Fair seeking capital to start other ventures, the South Pacific Coast was sold to the Southern Pacific. While service initially saw little change, pleas from local merchants, who were paying to reload their freight onto broad-gauge trains at San Jose, resulted in the extension of the wider, more universal gauge. The standard gauge was completed from San Jose to Los Gatos in 1895, though a third, inner rail would remain to accommodate the narrow-gauge trains that still provided through service on the line. Following both the Southern Pacific's hesitation and a three-year closure of the line following damage from the 1906 earthquake, the broad gauge was completed to Santa Cruz in 1909, at which point the inner rail was removed and the narrow-gauge equipment was disposed.

With the advent of Southern Pacific broad-gauge service, the line over the Santa Cruz Mountains continued to thrive. Now compatible with the rest of the area's railroads, the Southern Pacific could offer a direct rail service to San Francisco, eliminating the ferry transfer at Alameda. Los Gatos's bustling rail yards, once boasting six tracks, were as busy as ever. The aging single-stall enginehouse at Elm Street and Boone Lane was expanded and a new, larger turntable constructed on its north side.

The clanging of a trolley was first heard in Los Gatos on March 19, 1904, heralding the arrival of the San Jose-Los Gatos Interurban Railway Company. Traveling along today's Los Gatos Boulevard and Main Street, the line curved onto Santa Cruz Avenue, following Highway 9 into Saratoga. In 1905, Interurban Railway president Oliver Hale purchased 105 acres of the former Rancho San Antonio, from rifle heiress Sarah Pardee Winchester and her sister Isabelle Pardee Merriman, intending to extend the trolley into Los Altos and Palo Alto. After the company was absorbed into the Southern Pacific, the discontented Pardee sisters lost their litigation with the omnipotent railroad after attempting to rescind the deal they had made with the Interurban Railway. When surveyors arrived to mark the planned right-of-way only a short distance from the Pardee ranch house, the sisters followed behind, pulling out stakes.

The Southern Pacific's purchase of the San Jose-Los Gatos Interurban Railway, reorganized as the Peninsular Railway by 1909, would further improve rail service in Los Gatos. While the trolley would reach Palo Alto as planned, the proposed right-of-way also opened the opportunity for a more direct rail link between San Francisco and Santa Cruz, bypassing San Jose approximately nine miles to the west. Splitting SP's Peninsula mainline at Mayfield (later California Avenue), the line headed southwest through Los Altos, Cupertino, and Saratoga before reaching Vasona Junction, two and a half miles from the Los Gatos Depot. The Mayfield Cut-Off, or Los Altos Branch as it is sometimes known, was completed in April 1908. A second track for the interurban paralleled the line north of Congress Junction by 1909, with trolleys handling all local service on that corridor. Losing patronage to buses and private automobiles, the beloved trolley, which even offered special excursions simply to enjoy the vistas of "The Valley of Heart's Delight," vanished in 1933. The Mayfield Cut-Off, single tracked after the end of interurban service, remained intact until 1964. A substantial portion is still used today as Union Pacific's Vasona Industrial Lead.

The Santa Cruz line, like so many other branchline operations, took a hard hit during the 1930s. Once-bustling mountain hamlets such as Glenwood and Wrights became crumbling ghost towns, fading nearly as fast as they had sprouted up. While the loss of industry cut back freight traffic to one train a day in either direction, the growing popularity of the private automobile brought construction of Highway 17, offering travelers a more impromptu way to traverse the hill. In a final attempt to increase patronage, the Southern Pacific introduced the "Suntan Special"—a lengthy, often double-headed train that, in season, brought passengers from San Jose and San Francisco to the beach and boardwalk at Santa Cruz. Despite the success of the Suntan Special, which would outlast its original route, the line's days remained numbered.

Torrential rains wreaked havoc on the line in February 1940, spelling the end for the route. With little reason to justify the exorbitant cost of repairing the line, the Southern Pacific abandoned the approximately 16-mile portion between downtown Los Gatos and Olympia Station, north of Felton.

For the next 19 years, a local freight and the San Francisco–Mayfield–Los Gatos commute service continued to run into town. The SP's commercial steam era ended in 1957, and Los Gatos got a two-year taste of the modern diesel era before the rails were removed in January 1959 to their present terminus at Vasona Junction. Commute service in the West Valley was discontinued altogether in 1963 when the northern portion of the old Mayfield Cut-Off was removed to construct Foothill Expressway. The southern end of the line from Vasona to Simla Junction in Cupertino is used today by the Southern Pacific's successor, Union Pacific, to serve the Hanson cement plant at Permanente.

When the spikes were pulled in Los Gatos, a participant in the ceremony jokingly assured Los Gatans that they would not be left without a railroad, and he was right. A veteran of both the narrow- and standard-gauge rails over the Santa Cruz Mountains, legendary engineer Billy Jones ensured a railroading future for Los Gatos with the 1939 purchase of a forlorn miniature steam locomotive. Building the Wildcat Railroad at his Daves Avenue prune orchard, Jones ran the scaled-down pike for the enjoyment of himself and local children, giving the proceeds from his donation jar to local charitable causes. Following his death in 1968, devoted citizens honored Jones's legacy by forming a nonprofit organization to purchase and relocate the railroad to Oak Meadow and Vasona Parks. The organization continues to operate the train today. Since 1970, the little "2-Spot" has allowed nearly four generations to see and enjoy a real, operating steam locomotive.

More recent arrivals to Los Gatos may appreciate the lengthy downtown parking areas that run parallel to Santa Cruz and University Avenues, not realizing their automobiles are sitting on what was once railroad right-of-way. Many people have ridden the Billy Jones Wildcat Railroad in Oak Meadow Park, but they may not be aware of the true extent of his amazing story. This book preserves the names and deeds of Jones and others who contributed to the rich history of the railroads of Los Gatos.

For more than eight decades, the railroad was central to life in this town. Those who witnessed the railroads of Los Gatos will never forget the sights, sounds, and timeless romance of the steam locomotive. For all others, it is sincerely hoped that the photographs and stories presented here will convey why Los Gatos's railroads were so great.

One

THE RAILS REACH
LOS GATOS

Horse-drawn "hacks" meet a narrow-gauge train shortly after 1900. In 1877, town forefather, John Lyndon, deeded the land for the depot site to the railroad with the stipulation that his hotel be relocated across Santa Cruz Avenue. The 1899 Hotel Lyndon, seen at right, provided the background for many railroad photographs. (Courtesy Los Gatos Public Library.)

Heading south through Cats' Canyon, the rails crossed Los Gatos Creek three times, passing through the settlements of Alma, Lexington, and Wrights. Eight tunnels, with two more than a mile in length, were blasted through the mountains. Most tunnel labor was performed by Chinese laborers who, facing cave-ins and deadly gas explosions, risked their lives to place the Santa Cruz Mountains on track. (Courtesy Santa Clara City Library.)

In 1854, James Alexander Forbes built a stone mill on Los Gatos Creek, which finally flourished after 1870 as the Los Gatos Manufacturing Company. On its first entry into town, the South Pacific Coast was built past the mill on a grade along Los Gatos Creek, a plan quickly foiled by the discovery of unstable clay deposits. The final mainline alignment was established up the hill between University and Santa Cruz Avenues, but the remains from this first attempt served as an approximately half-mile industrial spur that split near University and Bentley Avenues. (Courtesy Los Gatos Public Library.)

12

The branchline that served the Los Gatos Manufacturing Company extended well beyond the old mill, running to a limestone quarry established to build Forbes' Mill more than two decades earlier. Narrow-gauge trains brought the stone to a kiln, located on Loma Alta Avenue, and later retrieved barrels for shipment behind what is today Old Town. When the president of the Los Gatos Manufacturing Company, William McMurtry, learned of the railroad's completion, he ordered 10 boxcars to the spur where they were promptly loaded with bags of flour. The spur, never broad-gauged, was removed by the 1920s. (Courtesy Los Gatos Public Library.)

Wrights Station, south of Alma and Lexington, was an important shipping point for local farmers. On July 4, 1885, Wrights burned to the ground. A boxcar served as a makeshift store and post office until the settlement could be rebuilt. In this c. 1893 photograph, growers are seen transferring their product from wagon to narrow-gauge boxcar. (Courtesy Los Gatos Public Library.)

South Pacific Coast No. 15 and crew rest at Los Gatos following a northbound run "over the hill." Built by the Baldwin Locomotive Works, No. 15 later served the North Pacific Coast trackage of the Northwestern Pacific, spending the remainder of its career in Marin and Sonoma Counties until scrapped in 1926. Posing with his family beside the stately 4-4-0 in 1884 is George Colgrove, former stagecoach driver and the railroad's second conductor. (Courtesy Los Gatos Public Library.)

Narrow-gauge boxcars wait to be loaded at the Los Gatos Canning Company, located between Santa Cruz and Lyndon Avenues. A spur that crossed Santa Cruz Avenue allowed shipment via rail and steamship to New York and England, however, it was necessary to transfer goods onto standard-gauge cars at San Jose, resulting in added fees. Pressure from the canneries contributed to the arrival of the standard gauge in 1895. (Courtesy Los Gatos Weekly Times; John Baggerly Collection.)

On May 1, 1891, Pres. Benjamin Harrison spoke succinctly from a decorated flatcar, commenting that the orchards and vineyards of the Santa Cruz Mountains "rival in productiveness the famous valleys of your state." After being presented with a basket of locally grown oranges, the president continued on his way. (Courtesy Los Gatos Public Library.)

This c. 1884 view shows the single-stall enginehouse and "gallows" turntable at Elm Street and Boone Lane. In the years of flourishing industry, Los Gatos was assigned its own switch engine—the first of which was a draft horse. A second stall and new turntable were added in 1899 to accommodate the larger standard-gauge locomotives. Both were gone by 1918. (Courtesy Los Gatos Public Library.)

Following nearly six months of negotiations, the South Pacific Coast was absorbed into the Southern Pacific empire in 1887. The slow conversion of the line to standard gauge began in 1894, and on September 7, 1895, standard-gauge No. 1370 became the first broad-gauge locomotive in Los Gatos. In 1899, the Southern Pacific held its annual employee picnic in Los Gatos, running five 10-car trains in on the broad gauge. (Courtesy Los Gatos Public Library.)

On April 15, 1900, hundreds turned out to welcome the first standard-gauge passenger train. While service to San Francisco no longer required the ferry, an across-the-platform transfer was necessary at San Jose during the earliest days of the broad gauge. When this photograph was taken, extension of the broad gauge past the "Gem City" had only been contemplated. (Courtesy Los Gatos Public Library.)

During its heyday at the turn of the century, Los Gatos was home to a bustling yard and both narrow- and standard-gauge trains passed through several times daily. These dapper Los Gatans will soon be enjoying the comfort of a plush narrow-gauge coach, the majority on the S.P.C. constructed by the Carter Brothers of Newark. Note the dual-gauge track. (Courtesy Los Gatos Public Library.)

A spit-and-polish, standard-gauge 4-6-0 participates in unknown 1909 festivities while the Grand Army of the Republic, an organization of Union veterans of the Civil War, executes a drill. In the background sits the Rankin Block, today home to Le Boulanger, and the Opera House, built by depot agent Eugene Long Ford in 1904. (Courtesy Museums of Los Gatos.)

Where roads meet rails, there is constant risk of danger. On March 29, 1906, a narrow-gauge train struck Lewis Shilling, "literally severing him in twain." The Southern Pacific constructed a manually operated crossing gate and a watchman's shanty on Main Street in 1910. It was replaced by automatic "wigwag" crossing signals in 1924. (Courtesy Los Gatos Public Library.)

Until the 1940s, Los Gatos provided a place for thirsty locomotives to "top off." The old water tank, pictured in this rare 1920s–1930s view, once stood beyond the freight shed at the far end of the yard. (Courtesy Elayne Shore Shuman.)

Broad gauging the line to Santa Cruz was a tremendous feat. In addition to relaying track, widening curves, strengthening and replacing bridges, and reboring tunnels, interference from nature provided challenges. The 1906 earthquake brought catastrophic damage to the line, halting all through traffic until it reopened as a standard-gauge road in May 1909. The inner rail, no longer needed, was removed by the time this c. 1910 photograph was taken. (Courtesy Los Gatos Public Library.)

Los Gatos's role as a "bedroom community" was predicted as early as May 1885, when the *Los Gatos News* reported, "Many persons who do business in San Francisco reside in the vicinity of Los Gatos." In 1907, the Mayfield Cut-Off was constructed between Los Gatos and the California Avenue station in Palo Alto, offering a more direct route to San Francisco via a nine-mile bypass of San Jose through Los Altos, Cupertino, and Saratoga. (Map by author.)

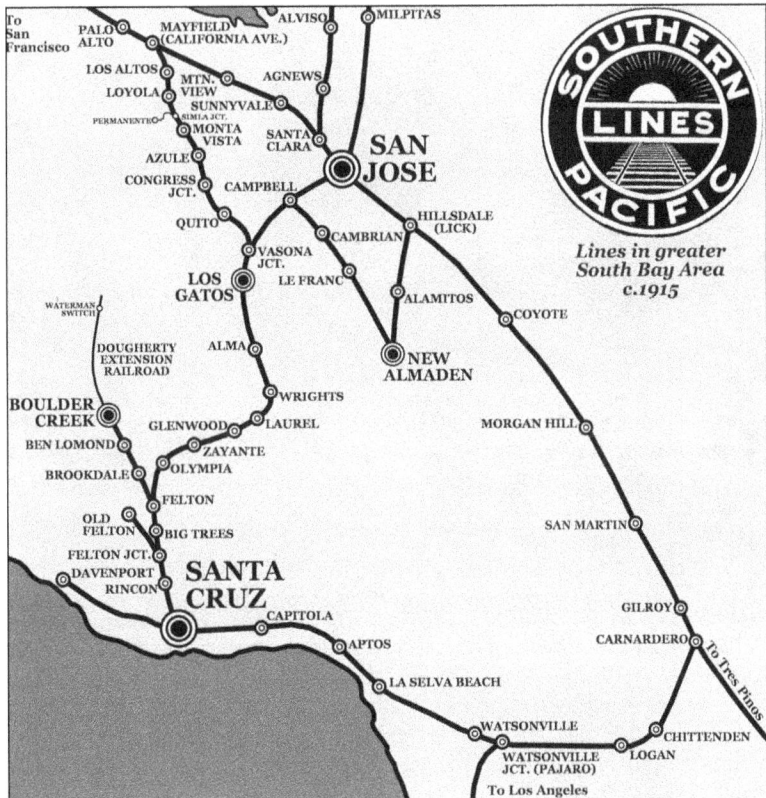

19

Train No. 84, the Monterey Local, heads into Cats' Canyon around 1920. Bound for Pacific Grove, it would reach Santa Cruz at 11:35 a.m., three and a half hours after departing San Francisco. No. 2304, a Class T-23 4-6-0, is on the point with a string of wooden coaches in tow. (Courtesy Los Gatos Public Library.)

Albert August Vollmer, a Pollard Road prune rancher, made the two-and-a-half-mile trip into town daily to transport his daughter, who commuted by train to San Jose. After years of traveling south for his daughter to catch a northbound train, Vollmer wrote the Southern Pacific suggesting a flag stop in his area, to which he received a favorable response. In honor of his childhood pony, Vollmer named the stop Vasona. Pictured here c. 1964, Vasona became the location where the Mayfield Cut-Off met the San Jose-Santa Cruz mainline. (Courtesy Jim Holmes.)

20

The Monterey Local passes through Wright, as the station was known during its later years. In 1932, the Southern Pacific closed the station, which had fostered mountain agriculture and played host to the celebrated "picnic trains." The site was later sold to San Jose Water Company. (Courtesy Museums of Los Gatos.)

Plans for a street railway in Los Gatos materialized as early as 1887, when local businessmen proposed running a trolley, horse car, or cable car line down Main Street and Santa Cruz Avenue. In 1902, James Rea and F. S. Granger incorporated the San Jose, Saratoga and Los Gatos Interurban Railway Company. Reorganized the following year as the San Jose-Los Gatos Interurban Railway, the company, fighting competition from San Jose railroads, completed their line to Los Gatos in March 1904. (Courtesy Los Gatos Public Library.)

San Jose-Los Gatos Car No. 11 rounds the bend at E. Main and Pleasant Streets, c. 1904. The interurban made its eastern entry into town via San Jose Road (Los Gatos Boulevard) and followed Main Street and Santa Cruz Avenue through the business district before heading for Saratoga via Highway 9. The El Monte Hotel, destroyed by fire in 1909, is visible in the background. (Courtesy Los Gatos Library and Museum History Project.)

An interurban car rolls past pedestrians, a parked automobile, and the E. E. Place funeral cart as it turns onto Santa Cruz Avenue, c. 1910. In 1909, the Peninsular Railway began service to Palo Alto, following the Mayfield Cut-Off north from Congress Junction. The trolley provided the only local service on the Mayfield line until interurban service ended and the second track was removed. (Courtesy Los Gatos Public Library.)

Peninsular Car No. 52 travels between Los Gatos and Saratoga, paralleling Highway 9 to the depot on Big Basin Way. From Saratoga, a one-and-a-half-mile branch line split off to reach Congress Springs while the mainline continued down Saratoga Avenue to its intersection with Stevens Creek Boulevard. Built by the American Car Company in 1903, Car No. 52 was one of two San Jose-Los Gatos cars preserved at the Western Railway Museum at Rio Vista Junction. (Courtesy Los Gatos Public Library.)

Rinconada, the Peninsular Railway stop at Kennedy and San Jose Roads, featured this Mission Revival–style passenger shed. The tracks continued down the center of San Jose Road and Bascom Avenue until they intersected the Southern Pacific's Campbell to New Almaden branch. For 1.64 miles, the trolley shared the branch's single-track right-of-way through Cambrian Park and Campbell, a portion that was briefly both dual gauge and electrified. (Courtesy Los Gatos Public Library.)

23

Peninsular Car No. 57 was one of many to jump the tracks at Austin Corners. At the intersection of Quito Road and Austin Way, fallen leaves, dampened by rainwater, frequently created slick conditions. Although the interurban was a traffic nightmare, it resulted in only one fatality in its nearly 30-year existence in town. (Courtesy Museums of Los Gatos.)

Sporting the later two-tone olive and cream paint scheme, a Peninsular car scoots down North Santa Cruz Avenue around 1930. While the rails curved onto Main Street, the track continuing straight in the foreground went across to the depot where cars would lay over beside SP trains. Competition from buses and private automobiles lead to the trolley's demise in 1933. (Courtesy Los Gatos Public Library.)

Two

TIMES ON THE
FRIENDLY RAILROAD

Los Gatos's pride in its railroad is reflected by this attractive (but inaccurate) postcard touting the "Los Gatos Streamliner." While streamlined steam rarely left the mainline, it ironically did make a brief appearance in Los Gatos over the winter of 1956, when Pacifics No. 2487 and No. 2489, which featured skyline casings, were tested on the San Francisco–Los Gatos commute. This 1920s–1930s era view captures Train No. 32, a Santa Cruz local, above what is now Vasona Park. (Courtesy Los Gatos Public Library.)

Los Gatos's depot was a modest structure. A December 1892 column in the *Los Gatos News* stated, "It is no uncommon thing to hear visitors remark, 'Well, if one is to judge of Los Gatos by the size and appearance of its passenger depot, it can't be much of a place.'" A baggage room was added in 1899, and in 1924, the aging edifice was heavily remodeled into this attractive Mission Revival structure. (Courtesy Los Gatos Public Library.)

A Santa Cruz–bound freight skirts around the Vasona Reservoir on March 11, 1939. 4-8-0 "Mastodons," such as No. 2923, were common power on freights over the mountains until the line's abandonment in 1940. (Photograph by Wil Whittaker; courtesy Eddie Chase.)

Alma, the station immediately south of Los Gatos, was once a bustling mountain hamlet, which experienced both birth and death by the timber industry. Little more than a residential community by the 1930s, it remained a flag stop until the abandonment of the line. The settlement was obliterated by the Lexington Reservoir project. (Photograph by Wil Whittaker; courtesy Eddie Chase.)

Workers unload a flatcar of telephone poles at the south end of Los Gatos Yard. Judging by the presence of a water column and absence of the interurban, this view was most likely captured in the late 1930s. Following the abandonment of the mountain line, watering facilities were no longer needed at Los Gatos and were removed by the mid-1940s. (Courtesy Chuck Bergtold.)

Dwindling patronage on Santa Cruz passenger service is evident by this two-car local, pictured above Vasona Reservoir in March 1939. Less than a year before the line would fade into history, the late Wilbur Whittaker photographed it almost in its entirety, camping trackside as he followed the scenic route on foot. (Photograph by Wil Whittaker; courtesy Eddie Chase.)

This late 1930s photograph provides an overview of the Los Gatos Depot and vicinity during the final days of Santa Cruz passenger service. Note the water tower, pictured in the background, and the landmark Town Plaza Christmas tree that was planted by the History Club of Los Gatos in 1923. The cement footing for one of the two semaphores pictured in the background still remains along a vacant, unpaved portion of the former right-of-way. (Courtesy Los Gatos Public Library.)

Chartered by 33 regulars on the San Francisco commute, the Los Gatos Commuter's Club was founded in March 1912. While its primary purpose was to lobby for schedule amendments and other service improvements, the club also sought to attract tourists and new residents to town, and in 1933 introduced its annual commuter's Christmas party on rails. (Courtesy Barbara Baggerly.)

BIGGER THAN EVER

LOS GATOS COMMUTERS AND Way Station Friends

PRESENT THEIR SIXTH ANNUAL

Christmas Celebration

FRIDAY, DECEMBER 22nd, 1939

Both ways on TRAIN, leaving Los Gatos at 6:49 A. M. and TRAIN leaving San Francisco at 5:17 P. M. TRAIN Stops at Redwood City on Return Trip.

THREE CARS—OUR OWN DECORATED CAR, PLUS Buffet and Espee's Special Dancing Car

A Non-Profit Party ● You Buy the Ticket ● We Furnish the Rest

Entertainment ● Prizes (Plenty) ● Group Singing A PRESENT FOR EACH AND EVERY ONE

★ **SPECIAL EVENTS** ★

Real Music by MR. ERLE GIBSON, Accordionist Extraordinary "You Name It—He Plays It" ● Dance as You Ride

Return Trip on the 5:17 P. M. Train ● Buffet Service with ALL that goes with it!

TICKETS LIMITED TO AVOID OVER-CROWDING, SO TAKE THE HINT AND

Buy Your Ticket Now!

DON'T MISS IT — A REAL PARTY Don't say, "I wish I had been with you"

ASK LAST YEAR'S CELEBRANTS!

The sixth annual Los Gatos Commuter's Christmas Party took to the rails in December 1941. Featuring live entertainment, dancing, and a buffet dinner, the commuter's club chartered three cars of the 5:17 p.m. train for the event, including this "Suburban" coach. "Way station friends" from Congress Junction, Azule, and other stops were also invited to join the festivities. (Courtesy Barbara Baggerly.)

Louis Chess, the Southern Pacific Company's general passenger agent, is pictured with Barbara Gibson of Los Gatos. Gibson, who later married local journalist John Baggerly, entertained the crowd with her vocal talents. (Courtesy Barbara Baggerly.)

The tip of the La Cañada turret can be seen in the background of this c. 1948 photograph, captured as a special prepares to leave town. Ten-wheelers such as the No. 2380 were not uncommon on the San Francisco commute service before Pacifics arrived by the late 1940s. (Photograph by Ralph Randol; courtesy Eddie Chase.)

Another railfan camera captured the same 1948 excursion, this view looking south across Main Street. Notice the depot garden, town Christmas tree, and a wigwag, the final incarnation of crossing protection at Main Street. (Courtesy Chuck Bergtold.)

After running around its train, 4-6-0 No. 2367 heads Train No. 185 back to San Jose, tender first. While the line to Santa Cruz was intact in this March 1939 view, this practice would become standard for all trains into Los Gatos the following year, when the 16-mile portion between Los Gatos and Olympia Station was abandoned. (Photograph by Wil Whittaker; courtesy Eddie Chase.)

No. 2829, among the regular power on Los Gatos–bound freights, runs light across Gray's Lane, likely heading to switch the Hunt Brothers Cannery and Standard Oil spurs. The homes to the left, which front University Avenue, today border the parking lot that occupies the former right-of-way. (Courtesy Tom Shreve; Charlie Ward collection.)

A short local freight, headed by 2-8-0 Consolidation No. 2781, backs towards Lark Avenue from Los Gatos in May 1955. The tank car has just been picked up from the Standard Oil spur at Farley Road. (Photograph by Jim Jefferson; courtesy Eddie Chase.)

Bound for the cement kilns above Cupertino, the Permanente Local drifts past orchards along Wedgewood Avenue on the Mayfield Cut-Off. The local, typically based from San Jose's Newhall Yard, would follow the cut-off to Simla Junction near Monta Vista where it would split onto Kaiser Cement Corporation's privately owned, 1.7-mile spur. Opened in 1939, the plant remains active today, justifying Union Pacific's continued operation of the Permanente Local. (Courtesy Eddie Chase collection.)

RIDE S.P'S "suntan special" to SANTA CRUZ BEACH SUNDAYS June 16-Sept. 1 (Also July 4)

JUNE JULY AUG SEPT.

$2.50 PLUS TAX ROUNDTRIP • KIDS UNDER 14, ½ fare • UNDER 6, FREE
LEAVE THIRD STREET STATION 8:17 a. m. • 6 HOURS AT THE BEACH

By the 1920s, most freight and passenger traffic had diminished over the Santa Cruz Mountains. In a moderately successful campaign to breathe life back into the line, the Southern Pacific introduced the seasonal "Suntan Special," offering a relaxing way for San Franciscans and San Joseans to escape to the beach and boardwalk at Santa Cruz. Unfortunately, it would prove only to postpone the inevitable. (Artwork by author, based on old SP advertisement.)

4-8-0 No. 2923 leads a Santa Cruz–bound freight over the first Los Gatos Creek bridge. Torrential rains during the winter of 1940 brought Southern Pacific to abandon the 16-mile portion of the line between downtown Los Gatos and Olympia Station, ending 60 years of service through the Santa Cruz Mountains. (Photograph by Wil Whittaker.)

A steam crane prepares to remove the first Los Gatos Creek bridge south of town in June 1940. The tracks leading up to the span's former location remained in place for several years and were used to deliver concrete culverts when the creek was dammed to flood Cats' Canyon. (Courtesy Railway Negative Exchange; Warren Edward Miller Collection.)

While the iron artery over "the hill" had been severed, Los Gatos industries kept the freights rolling through town. In the 1940s, freight traffic was provided by the Sewall S. Brown and Hunt Brothers canneries, Standard Oil on Farley Road, the winery at Sacred Heart Novitiate, and Sterling Lumber Company on University Avenue. (Courtesy Eddie Chase.)

2-8-0 No. 2788 passes through the north leg of Vasona Wye on trackage still used today by the Union Pacific. The Sewall S. Brown Cannery, located where Highway 85 now crosses beneath the tracks, is visible in the background. (Courtesy Jim Holmes.)

Just past Vasona Junction, No. 2781 leads a local freight toward town in this c. 1949 view. (Courtesy Eddie Chase.)

Consolidation No. 2781 crosses Winchester Boulevard on the south leg of Vasona Wye. While long gone from this location, the historic watchmen's shanty at Vasona was rescued by Jim and Dick Holmes and survives today alongside their 15-inch gauge live steam logging railroad in the Santa Cruz Mountains. (Courtesy Jim Holmes.)

Two boxcars, one of which toppled onto the bed of a pickup truck, jumped the tracks at Farley Road in 1956. It was possibly the last, but certainly not the first, derailment in Los Gatos. On December 24, 1906, a Santa Cruz–bound train jumped the tracks past Vasona following heavy rains. If not for steel coaches, far more serious casualties would have occurred when cars slid down the banks of Los Gatos Creek. (Photograph by Charlie Ward; courtesy Phil Reader.)

A wrecking train, headed by 2-8-0 No. 2625, creeps towards Vasona Junction. For reasons of visibility, the Southern Pacific painted their smoke-box fronts silver in the mid-1940s. (Courtesy Eddie Chase.)

"Mikado" No. 3255 was among the largest freight locomotives to run into Los Gatos, pictured here approaching the Saratoga Avenue (Los Gatos-Saratoga Road) crossing on May 15, 1947. The superlative, said to be Class F-1 2-10-2s, were used briefly on the branch in the 1940s, a claim substantiated by the late Al Smith and Neil Vodden. (Photograph by Jim Jefferson; courtesy Eddie Chase.)

2-8-2 No. 3251, believed to be the last operating Mikado on the entire Southern Pacific system, leads the final steam freight into Los Gatos on September 19, 1956. Steam power would remain on the commute service until January 1957. (Photograph by Jim Jefferson; courtesy Eddie Chase.)

A steam freight arrives at the Los Gatos Depot for the last time, posing beside the old freight shed built nearly 80 years earlier by the South Pacific Coast. This was the end of an era not only in Los Gatos but also in the entire Bay Area. (Photograph by Jim Jefferson; courtesy Eddie Chase.)

After discharging its passengers, the Los Gatos commutes deadheaded back to San Jose, where they would be serviced and stored overnight. While this photograph depicts the weekday evening deadhead turning on Vasona Wye, typical practice was to run around the train at Los Gatos, taking the nine-mile trip to San Jose tender first. Regulars on the run were fitted with rear pilots for this reason. (Courtesy Eddie Chase.)

A Peerless Stages bus meets Train No. 170, the San Francisco–Los Gatos commute, at Vasona Junction. Following the abandonment of the mountain line, Peerless, which maintained a depot on North Santa Cruz Avenue, operated a bus connection from the depot to Santa Cruz. (Courtesy Eddie Chase.)

After a turn on the wye, an atypical procedure, the deadhead continues its run back to San Jose along Winchester Boulevard in Campbell. P-1 Class "Pacific" No. 2401 was among the older 4-6-2s on the Southern Pacific system, rebuilt in the late 1920s to a Class P-4 at the railroad's Los Angeles General Shops. (Courtesy Eddie Chase.)

Three

LEGENDARY RAILROADER AND HIS PRUNE ORCHARD PIKE

William "Billy" Jones would make his humble entry into the world on January 26, 1884. Fascinated by the colorful, cinder-belching beasts that rolled through his hometown of Ben Lomond, Jones, having completed his formal education at 13, sought employment to assist his struggling family. He was hired as an engine wiper at the South Pacific Coast's Boulder Creek roundhouse. Four decades later, his seniority would earn him a spot on the most coveted run the railroad had to offer—the Coast Daylight. (Southern Pacific Company photograph; courtesy Jones family.)

Billy Jones moved quickly through the ranks of the South Pacific Coast. He was soon promoted to hostler, responsible for lighting off, fueling, lubricating, and performing any needed light maintenance on locomotives before the first run of the day. Entering engine service as a fireman at age 17, he was promoted to engineer by 21. (Courtesy Jones family.)

Among Jones's regular assignments were runs down the South Pacific Coast's two major branch lines, Felton–Boulder Creek and Campbell–New Almaden, to San Jose. Jones was among the first to receive a transfer to broad gauge, working out of the Lenzen Avenue roundhouse in San Jose. In this c. 1915 view, Jones is pictured beside No. 1380's pilot at bottom right. (Courtesy Jones family.)

Fate played its hand one day when a group of railroaders, including Billy Jones, tied up their work train for lunch at Wright's Station. While awaiting his meal, Jones approached the hamlet's young schoolteacher, Geraldine McGrady, a meeting that eventually led to their marriage on June 26, 1918. The young couple settled in San Luis Obispo, where Billy was assigned to the helper engines over Cuesta Grade. They would later return to the nine-acre prune orchard Jones had purchased at Daves Avenue and Winchester Boulevard. (Courtesy Jones family.)

Geraldine McGrady Jones, pictured to the left of her husband, began her job at Wright's one-room schoolhouse in 1914. A 1911 graduate of Los Gatos High School, she pursued her teacher training at San Jose State Normal School (San Jose State University), commuting from her family's Los Gatos home via the Peninsular Railway. (Courtesy Jones family.)

Clad in his trademark ivy cap, Billy Jones poses with his fireman beside a Daylight locomotive. The run over Cuesta Grade was the most grueling stretch of mainline on the Coast Division, with longer trains, such as the Daylight, requiring helper engines up the more than three-percent climb. GS-class locomotives sported such modern appurtenances as the high-water alarm, which would trigger an automatic surface (steam dome) blowdown should the water level reach what was deemed "too high." Jones's opinion of these devices was no secret and, in order to make the grade, he was known to render them inoperable. One notable story involved a company inspector riding in the cab who, upon responding to Jones's routine procedure in outrage, was encouraged to try the run himself. The highfalutin "brass hat" obliged and, after triggering a blowdown and stalling the gargantuan 4-8-4 on the hill, was never seen by Jones again. (Courtesy Jones family.)

Late in 1918, Billy Jones took a San Jose–Watsonville assignment. After the birth of their first daughter, Betty, the Joneses were again uprooted with an assignment to San Luis Obispo. By the time they returned to Los Gatos, the family had grown to include two sons. Daughter Geraldine completed the family soon after. In this August 1942 photograph, Billy poses with sons Bob and Neal at the University of California while Bob was on leave from the Army Air Corps. Neal attended Berkeley for six months until he too enlisted. (Courtesy Jones family.)

To pass time during layovers, Billy Jones would walk the docks along the San Francisco waterfront. In 1939, Jones discovered a forlorn miniature steam locomotive in a warehouse hours before it was to be shipped to Japan as scrap metal. Telling the dealer he would place his mailbox on it, Jones purchased the engine for $100 and had it trucked to his ranch in Los Gatos. That very locomotive is pictured here at a Long Beach scrap yard in 1936. (Courtesy California State Railroad Museum.)

Eccentric millionaire Abbott Kinney sought to recreate picturesque Venice, Italy, along the Southern California Coast. Seeking a unique transportation system for his community, Kinney called upon John Coit, a civil engineer who built and operated an 18-inch gauge steam railway in Los Angeles's Eastlake Park. Using his 2-6-0 as a prototype, Coit set to work designing an oil-fired 2-6-2 Prarie-type locomotive, two of which would be built at Los Angeles's Johnson Machine Works in 1905. The innovative design utilized an unusual cylindrical firebox (or "Vanderbilt") boiler and Walschaerts valve gear, which at that time had yet to see widespread popularity on its full-scale counterparts. (Courtesy Phil Reader.)

Venice Railway Nos. 1 and 2 lead a doubleheader in this undated photograph. During busy periods, John Coit would bring out Engine No. 1903 from his Eastlake Park operation, which became the honorary VMR No. 3. Doubleheaders with the *Mogul* and one of her larger sisters were not uncommon, but those with both Prairies on point were a somewhat less frequent occurrence. (Courtesy Phil Reader.)

46

Taken during the later part of her career on the Venice Railway, this photograph reveals a tired 2-Spot after the replacement of the original spoked pilot and trailing wheels. John Coit, whose frustration with Abbott Kinney and his business antics lead to a bitter falling out, left the Venice Railway by 1915. Due to poor ridership and opposition by local merchants, the Venice Railway ceased operation in February 1925. (Courtesy Phil Reader.)

The remains of the Venice Railway passed through a succession of Southern California scrap dealers for more than a decade. In 1935, a San Gabriel man discovered Engine No. 1 at a Vernon junkyard and purchased it, along with a tender, four coaches, the turntable, and some rail, for $950. While the 2-spot was separated from the lot at an unknown point in time, its tender was the one purchased with the No. 1 at Vernon, explaining its tenderless reemergence in San Francisco four years later. (Courtesy Phil Reader.)

When Billy Jones purchased the little 2-Spot, he intended to build a backyard railroad he could operate with his two sons. Determined to return his engine to steam, Jones attended night school to acquire the needed skills, putting in many long hours at his company's Mission Bay Shops and constructing a tender using a fuel oil delivery tank. On August 13, 1942, Jones steamed up the 2-spot for the first time. Son Neal and daughter Geraldine were on hand to share this special moment on the ranch. (Courtesy Jones family.)

Acquiring rail from fruit dry yards across Santa Clara Valley, the Jones family and friends built a winding pike for the 2-Spot around the Daves Avenue prune orchard. Billy Jones's hunt for rolling stock and expertise led him to Louis M. MacDermot, builder of the 1/3-scale, 19-inch gauge Overfair Railway at the 1915 Panama-Pacific International Exposition in San Francisco. On October 16, 1943, MacDermot, pictured left of Jones, had the honor of driving the golden spike on the Wildcat Railroad. (Courtesy Jones family.)

The Golden Spike ceremony saw many local dignitaries in attendance, including Southern Pacific brass, a Bank of America representative, and the minister of the Jones's church. A decorated 2-Spot poses for a formal photograph during the ceremony, which commenced at 3:30 p.m. (Courtesy Jones family).

In November 1943, less than a month after the Golden Spike ceremony, the Joneses were informed that their son Bob had been killed in a plane crash over Alaska. Less than one year later, their son Neal died when his plane went down over the Philippines. While grief-stricken, Billy Jones stood strong and continued to build his Wildcat Railroad as a memorial to his two fallen sons. (Courtesy Jones family.)

Billy Jones takes the 2-Spot around one of the many curves on the orchard pike. Winchester Boulevard, then San Jose-Santa Clara Road, is seen in the background. (Courtesy Jones family.)

Billy Jones highballs out of the original Wildcat Depot, built of prune drying trays. In this early 1950s view, the 2-Spot has just received a fresh coat of orange, red, and black "Daylight" paint, just like the gargantuan "Golden States" Jones ran down the coast to San Luis Obispo. While this colorful scheme earned the Daylight its title as "the most beautiful train in the world," its aesthetic contributions on the 2-Spot were questionable. (Courtesy Jones family.)

The Brotherhood of Locomotive Engineers was represented by this float in San Jose's 1947 Labor Day Parade. Billy Jones, accompanying the 2-Spot as the parade moves down First Street, retired from the Southern Pacific two years later, ending a 60-year career. Following the parade, Jones displayed the 2-Spot at the Santa Clara County Fair, the first held since the end of World War II. (Courtesy Barbara Phinney; BJWRR collection.)

A passenger coach, built by Louis MacDermot in 1915, rounds a bend on the Wildcat Railroad. MacDermot learned of plans to hold an exposition to celebrate the Panama Canal opening and San Francisco's recovery from the 1906 earthquake. Believing a scaled-down version of a modern, mainline steam passenger railroad would be a fitting transportation system on the exposition grounds, he turned to his affluent family for backing who, despite much skepticism, agreed to fund the venture. (Courtesy Jim Holmes.)

MacDermot's Oakland estate became home to a bustling locomotive shop where crews built five 1/3-scale, 19-inch gauge steam locomotives. A 0-6-0T tank engine, No. 1500, was followed by four exquisite Pacifics based on the SP's ALCO (Brooks)-built Class P-6. Only No. 1500 and Pacifics 1912, 1913, and 1914 would see operation, while No. 1915 was never completed. MacDermot's workmanship earned them the reputation of being among the finest miniature locomotives ever constructed. (Courtesy California State Railroad Museum.)

While an astounding 18 million filed through the gates of the Panama-Pacific International Exposition, MacDermot's Overfair Railway was a complete bust. As management would warrant only a "dogbone" layout toward the rear of the grounds, few patrons ever knew of its existence. Furthermore, a steam train, even a scaled-down one, wasn't a novelty in 1915—it was a common sight in everyday life. (Courtesy California State Railroad Museum.)

Following the exposition, the Overfair Railway's entire roster returned to the MacDermot estate, where it would remain in storage for nearly three decades. Plans to run the locomotives along the old North Pacific Coast right-of-way in Marin and Sonoma Counties and at the 1939–1940 Treasure Island World's Fair never reached fruition. (Courtesy California State Railroad Museum.)

Cut off from his family fortune, MacDermot became increasingly eccentric and let his estate fall into disrepair. In the early 1940s, MacDermot arranged for what would prove to be a short-lived operation of No. 1913 at the Oakland Zoo. After losing their Oakland estate, MacDermot and his wife moved into the apartment above Billy Jones's garage. (Courtesy Jones family.)

To financially assist MacDermot, Jones purchased the remaining roster of the Overfair Railway, including all five locomotives. In the photograph above, Engine No. 1500 poses on the turntable while the 2-Spot simmers in the background. After his wife's death, an impoverished MacDermot was taken in by the Hoyle family of Wilder Avenue. Spending his final days in the backyard playhouse, the great machinist died on February 22, 1948. (Courtesy Jones family.)

Inspired by studio colleagues, such as Ward Kimball and Ollie Johnson, Walt Disney became interested in taking up live steam as a hobby. Upon hearing of Jones's growing stable of scale-iron horses, the legendary showman and his friends arranged to pay "Casey" Jones a visit at his Los Gatos orchard. Disney, along with Ward Kimball, Eddie Sergeant, and Roger Broggie, flew to San Francisco and headed south by limousine. A local gas station attendant phoned the press after the chauffeur requested directions to the Jones ranch. Following a hearty breakfast prepared by Geraldine Jones, Disney and friends enjoyed a day of running the 2-Spot. (Courtesy Jones family.)

In 1949, Disney became the owner of his own 1 1/2-inch scale, 7 1/4-inch gauge live steam locomotive, the *Lilly Belle*. Upon completion of his backyard Carolwood Pacific railroad, Disney invited Billy and Geraldine Jones to visit his Holmby Hills estate. Reminiscent of the ornate locomotives on which he first began his career, Jones displays a wide grin as he takes the little teakettle for a run. (Courtesy Jones family.)

Walt Disney and Geraldine Jones pose beside Disney's famous "Dancing Man," the prototype to the audio animatronics technology that defined Disney theme parks. The idea for Disneyland came when Disney, who opened his Carolwood Pacific for rides every weekend, sought a more suitable place to operate his railroad for the public. Disney wanted a place "like nothing else in the world . . . surrounded by a train." (Courtesy Jones family.)

56

Jones turned down Disney's offers to purchase the MacDermot locomotives, but the two remained friends. When Disneyland and its narrow-gauge railroad opened in July 1955, Jones was an "honorary engineer." He received a lifetime pass to the park, along with generous Christmas baskets every year. During his visit to the Disney estate, Jones is seen to the right while Paul Holsinger manually pumps water into the boiler of the *Lilly Belle*. Disney is at center. (Courtesy *Los Gatos Weekly-Times*; John Baggerly collection.)

Billy Jones poses beside No. 1500, the only Overfair locomotive to see attempted operation on the Wildcat. While the Pacifics stood no chance on the line's tight curves, Jones was willing to re-gauge his entire railroad to test the tank engine. He hastily did so in about a week and fired up No. 1500 alone one night. The derailed engine was brought back to the shop the next day, and the railroad returned to 18-inch gauge. (Courtesy Jones family.)

In pursuit of vacuum brake components, Billy Jones traveled to England and purchased another 18-inch gauge steam locomotive, the *Gwen*, built by the Hunslet Engine Company of Leeds. The *Gwen* was not a miniature, but a full-scale industrial locomotive built in 1920 for the John Knowles Company of Woodville, Burton-on-Trent, England. Sold in 1961, it has since been restored to museum-quality operating condition by its current owner. (Courtesy Eddie Chase.)

Like MacDermot, Billy Jones was unsuccessful in his pursuit of a permanent home for the Overfair equipment. His most promising idea was to sell it to the city of San Jose for use on the old Peninsular Railway grade through Alum Rock Park. The Town of Los Gatos, anxious to take advantage of its new downtown parking, was less receptive to the idea of a "Shopper's Special" down the recently abandoned Southern Pacific right-of-way. (Courtesy Jones family.)

Frederic "Cap" Shaw of Sausalito captured this shot for *Little Railways of the World*, his 1958 book documenting the history of miniature railroads. In 1961, Overfair Corporation, consisting of Shaw, Quentin Jervis, and a third silent partner, acquired the English engine *Gwen*, along with Overfair Locomotives 1500, 1914, and 1915. Moved to Jervis's San Pedro warehouse, only No. 1500 would eventually see brief operation at the Orange County Fairgrounds. (Courtesy California State Railroad Museum.)

"Whoops!" Billy Jones assesses a minor derailment that, luckily, put only the 2-Spot on the ground. While other bystanders, particularly railroaders, might have reacted to the situation with more colorful language, Jones had a penchant for never cursing. (Courtesy Jones family.)

On March 22, 1956, Billy Jones's enginehouse was destroyed in a raging inferno. Faulty wiring and an abundance of oily rags likely ignited the blaze, which destroyed original MacDermot patterns, Jones's collection of South Pacific Coast car lamps, and caused serious damage to the 2-Spot. Since the ranch was outside town limits, the nearest ladder company that would respond was in Alma. (Courtesy Barbara Phinney; BJWRR collection.)

A band of volunteers hose soot and ash off the 2-Spot after the devastating 1956 fire. The tender of the Holmes brothers' full-scale Heisler locomotive, the *Elk*, is pictured at right. While the original cab, removed in this photograph, was saved, the Venice Railway headlight was destroyed. (Courtesy Barbara Phinney; BJWRR collection.)

Contributing time, money, or services, the community reached out to help Billy Jones after the fire. While local contractors were hard at work constructing a new enginehouse, the Southern Pacific brought the badly damaged 2-Spot to their Bayshore Shops for rebuilding. In the photograph above, members of the Aahmes Temple Shrine present a check to Jones. (Courtesy Tom Shreve; Charlie Ward collection.)

Volunteers build the new station and enginehouse in the background while Billy Jones paints the red stripe of the famed Daylight scheme on the 2-Spot's new boiler jacket. The locomotive had recently returned from the SP's Bayshore Shops where it received significant mechanical work and a new set of flues. (Courtesy Tom Shreve; Charlie Ward collection.)

More than a dozen volunteers are pictured constructing the new station and enginehouse at the ranch. Few local organizations have ever achieved a following quite like the Wildcat Railroad, both in its days at the Jones orchard and in Oak Meadow Park. (Courtesy Jones family.)

This photograph depicts the Wildcat Railroad yard following reconstruction after the 1956 fire. The Wildcat's small turntable, sans added decking, was originally built to turn push cars in local fruit dry yards. The old water tower was built using a wine tank salvaged from a local vineyard. (Courtesy Jim Holmes.)

During the restoration effort of a full-scale, narrow-gauge Heisler locomotive at the ranch, the *Elk*, Billy Jones became somewhat envious of the beautiful wooden pilot, or "cowcatcher," Jim Holmes had built for it. Challenging himself to complete a carpentry project of his own, Jones built this homely little "crummy" from an Overfair Railway flatcar. (Courtesy Jones family.)

Every railroad has its fair share of mishaps, and the Wildcat Railroad was no exception. Top heavy and prone to rocking, especially with the encouragement of excited young passengers, Jones's homebuilt caboose was always of concern. On May 13, 1956, the caboose tipped on its side and skidded down a five-foot embankment, crushing the cupola. Luckily the only injury was a broken arm. (Courtesy Jim Holmes.)

Jim Holmes and Neil Vodden run the 2-Spot by a passing automobile (left) shortly after the fire as evidenced by the absence of tender lettering. In 1955, the 500-foot portion of the line parallel to Winchester Boulevard was moved approximately 20 feet to allow construction of two additional lanes. (Courtesy Tom Shreve; Charlie Ward collection.)

The commemorative passes Jones issued to special guests featured this impressionistic map (right) of the original Wildcat Railroad. (Courtesy Jones family.)

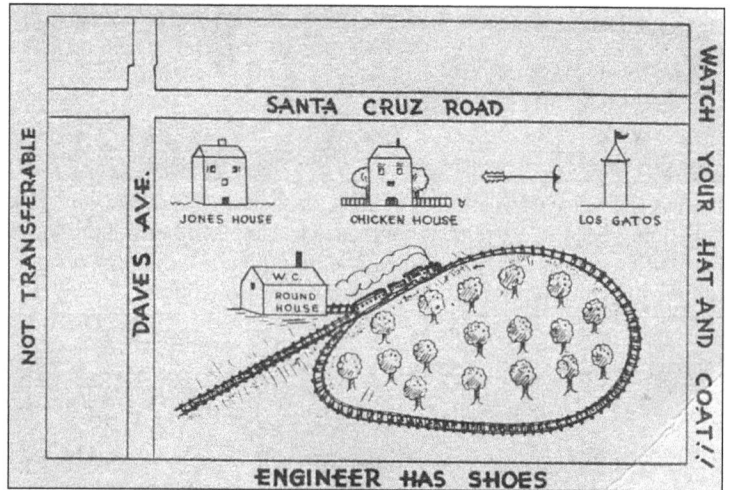

SANTA CRUZ ROAD

NOT TRANSFERABLE

WATCH YOUR HAT AND COAT!!

DAVES AVE.

JONES HOUSE

CHICKEN HOUSE

LOS GATOS

W.C. ROUND HOUSE

ENGINEER HAS SHOES

Billy Jones (left) welcomes visitors to the railroad's first day of the 1957 season. Every Sunday during the spring and summer months, the 2-Spot's shrill whistle drew children away from their Sunday chores. Jones never charged for rides, paying for fuel and other costs out of his own pocket. While a pickle jar sat out to collect donations, the contents typically went to local charities, particularly those benefiting children. On one occasion, an anonymous donor paid to refurnish the entire pediatric wing of Valley Medical Center. (Courtesy Tom Shreve; Charlie Ward collection.)

Accompanied by a young "cab" rider, Charlie Ward and Neil Vodden run the 2-Spot past the remains of a decaying Overfair Railway passenger car. The homebuilt coach Jones constructed from an Overfair flatcar is just visible to the right. (Courtesy Jim Holmes.)

Billy Jones takes the 2-Spot for a run during the early days of the Wildcat. Before serving in the military, high-school-aged Charlie Hoyle refitted the MacDermot coaches, seen in tow, with their automatic braking systems. (Courtesy Jones family.)

Excited passengers take whatever seat they can find on the train. Like the attractive roofed coaches, the freight cars had been constructed in 1915 for Louis MacDermot's Overfair Railway. (Courtesy Tom Shreve; Charlie Ward collection.)

The 2-Spot, adorned in Daylight colors, simmers at the depot while passengers from across the Santa Clara Valley file onto passenger coaches. The old bell, which once guarded the crossing at Vasona Junction, now sits atop a full-scale crossbuck in Vasona Park. (Courtesy Jones family.)

Blossoming prune trees and a looming Mount Umunhum provide a bucolic backdrop for this *c.* 1951 view. The guest fireman, clad in a fedora hat, is believed to be a Southern Pacific official, one of many to ride the little railroad. It is said one such visitor took notice of the numerous SP-marked tools in the Wildcat enginehouse. (Courtesy Jones family.)

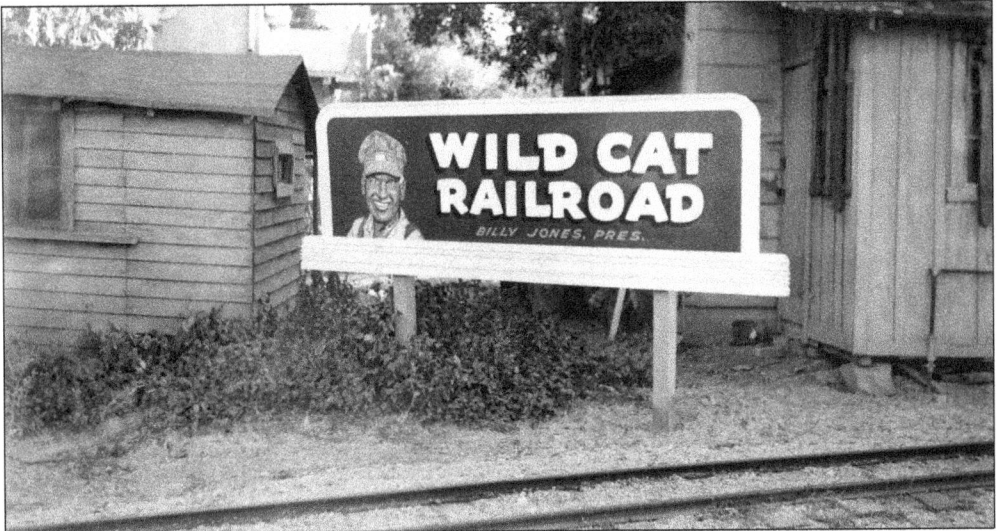

This scaled-down billboard was one of two that decorated the Wildcat right-of-way. While this one featured a likeness of Jones himself, the other was done up in typical SP advertising style. (Courtesy California State Railroad Museum.)

Visitors' cars can be seen lining the road as the 2-Spot, highballing out of the depot, makes its rounds at the Jones ranch. For nearly 25 years, a Sunday ride on the Wildcat was a Los Gatos tradition. When the Wildcat shut down for the winter in October 1967, few realized it would be the beginning of the end for the popular prune orchard pike. (Courtesy Jones family.)

On January 10, 1968, at the age of 83, Billy Jones passed away after a brief battle with leukemia. A kind-hearted and giving man who experienced his share of tragedy, Jones embraced life, enjoying it to its fullest. A true railroading legend, he left behind two daughters, five grandchildren, and a legacy that will ensure the survival of the railroad in Los Gatos for years to come. (Courtesy Jim Holmes.)

Four

PEOPLE OF THE RAILS

Countless individuals have contributed to the railroading legacy of Los Gatos. This c. 1988 photograph includes key players in the preservation of Billy Jones's Wildcat Railroad. Posed on the Oak Meadow turntable, from left to right, are Myron Alexander, a Campbell realtor; Bill Ulleseit, a power plant engineer at Valley Medical Center; Bill Mason, a longtime Los Gatan and electrical contractor; and Neil Vodden, a former Southern Pacific steam engineer. (Courtesy *Los Gatos Weekly-Times*; John Baggerly collection.)

William "Bill" Mason was the guiding force behind the Wildcat Railroad's relocation. A Los Gatos electrical contractor, he proposed the idea of a Billy Jones memorial in a letter to the *Los Gatos Times-Observer* stating, "No single man entertained more children from 2-to-60 in this valley than Billy Jones." When his proposition gained momentum, Mason became president of the nonprofit organization founded to relocate and operate the railroad. (Courtesy *Los Gatos Weekly-Times*; John Baggerly collection.)

When Bill Mason and others proposed saving Billy Jones's railroad, Barbara Phinney was already hard at work, clipping newspapers to document the historic move to Oak Meadow Park. The railroad's official historian, Phinney has spent the past 38 years creating, expanding, and organizing the railroad's historical file. (Courtesy Barbara Phinney; BJWRR collection.)

Neil Vodden's interest in railroading began at his childhood home on University Avenue. The sound of a whistle would be a cue for Vodden, often accompanied by his friend Charlie Hoyle, to grab his bicycle and ride to the depot where his father, a Railway Express employee, could often be found conversing with engine crews. Vodden laid track at Billy Jones' ranch during high school and, in 1944, was hired as a Southern Pacific fireman after Jones recommended his young apprentice. (Photograph by Charlie Ward; courtesy Phil Reader.)

Promoted to engineer in 1954, Neil Vodden served the Northwestern Pacific before being bumped to the two commute routes out of San Francisco, his favorite assignment being P-8 Pacific No. 2472. Vodden retired as a senior engineer on Amtrak's Coast Starlight in 1986. He played an active role in the restoration of No. 2472 at the San Mateo County Fairgrounds, serving as its regular engineer on mainline excursions until his death in 1997. (Courtesy Jim Holmes.)

Another of the "last generation" steam railroaders produced by Los Gatos, Charlie "The Hat" Hoyle was among the more colorful characters working for the Southern Pacific, though color blindness prevented him from ever serving on the road. A hostler and mechanic at the SP's San Jose and Oakland roundhouses, Hoyle later proved his artistry behind the throttle at Norman Clark's Roaring Camp and Big Trees tourist operation, which was free of block signals. (Courtesy Tom Shreve; Charlie Ward collection.)

A first-rate mechanic, Charlie Hoyle helped move SP Pacific No. 2467, the "pet" of Oakland roundhouse crews, for display at Harrison Park, enabling its return to operation years later. Known for his cantankerous disposition and "creative language," Hoyle's knowledge and careful guidance earned him the respect of all who worked with him. He made his final run up Bear Mountain in the cab of RC&BT No. 1, *Dixiana*, little more than a week before his death on December 25, 1986. This 1980s photograph was taken beside Overfair No. 1913 at Al Smith's Swanton Pacific Railroad. (Courtesy Phil Reader.)

A native of San Francisco, Charles Ward made a significant mark on Los Gatos railroading history. An artist, photographer, and Southern Pacific steam fireman, he served the 712th Railway Battalion, based out of Fort Eustis, Virginia, during the Korean War. In Seoul, Ward in essence became foreman of the Yongsan roundhouse, developing a particular affinity for a 1919 Baldwin Mikado, which he named "Mt. Tamalpais." A good friend of Neil Vodden and Charlie Hoyle, Ward later moved to Los Gatos and became a regular at Billy Jones's ranch. (Courtesy Tom Shreve; Charlie Ward collection.)

Visionary F. Norman Clark arrived in Felton with dreams of recreating a logging railroad of the 1880s, and Charlie Ward would play a major part of making this dream a reality. Ward sketched the railroad's herald, which features the Santa Cruz Railway No. 3 "Jupiter" on a trestle, when Clark's plans were to repatriate the historic locomotive to the area. Under Ward's supervision, Clark's 1912 Shay locomotive was transformed into Roaring Camp & Big Trees No. 1, the ornate "Dixiana." Ward, pictured in the cab of the "Dixie," fulfilled a lifelong dream with a move to Chile, a retirement sadly cut short in 1989 by a fatal spider bite. (Charlie Ward collection; courtesy Tom Shreve.)

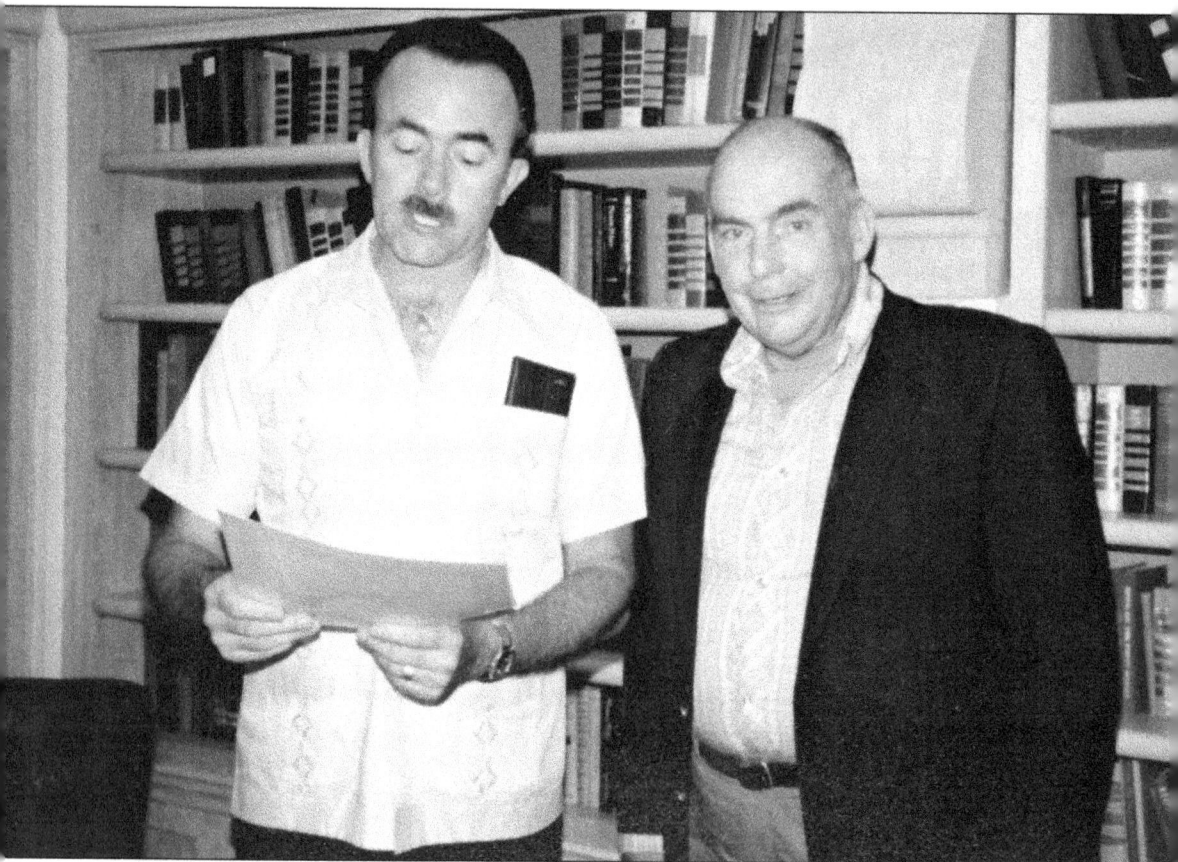

The late Albert B. "Al" Smith, pictured at right, was among Los Gatos's most beloved residents. After his brief career as a Southern Pacific brakeman was cut short by accident, Smith turned his attention to the family business—Orchard Supply Hardware. His success enabled him to establish a permanent home for MacDermot's Overfair Railway equipment at his Santa Cruz County ranch, where he constructed his two-mile Swanton Pacific Railroad. Smith also served as a Los Gatos councilman and mayor in 1977–1978. His love of railroading is reflected by the Orchard Supply railroad calendar, painted for many years by Mike Kotowski, who is pictured at left. Kotowski, a longtime BJWRR supporter and one-time Campbell mayor, is also credited as the creator of the railroad's "Billy Cat" herald along with its predecessor, "Sylvester." (Courtesy Barbara Phinney; BJWRR collection.)

Bill Ulleseit's involvement with the Billy Jones Wildcat Railroad began more than 50 years ago, when he and his wife stumbled upon Billy Jones's ranch on a weekend drive. After meeting Jones, Ulleseit offered to assist the affable hogger with weekend operations, something he continued to do until his death in 1968. Ulleseit, along with Southern Pacific fireman and master machinist Severn Edmonds, completely rebuilt the tired 2-Spot before the new railroad opened at Oak Meadow Park. He, his son, and his grandson are all involved with the railroad. (Courtesy Barbara Phinney; BJWRR collection.)

Pictured is the first board of directors of the Billy Jones Wildcat Railroad, Inc. Included here, from left to right, are (first row) Wint Smith, Myron Alexander, and Joe Whelan; (second row) Russell Cooney, Betty de Paolo, Bill Mason, Mike Kotowski, David Adams, and Jerry Kennedy. (Courtesy Barbara Phinney; BJWRR collection.)

Phil Reader's career as a steam locomotive mechanic began in 1978 when, under the tutelage of Neil Vodden, he became a regular engineer on the BJWRR—a role he would serve for nearly 15 consecutive summers. Reader, who is said to have more throttle time on the 2-Spot than Billy Jones himself, has since moved on to serve the Roaring Camp & Big Trees, Sierra Railroad, the former Georgetown Loop Railroad, Inc. of Colorado, and the Pacific Coast Railroad in Santa Margarita. Other Wildcat "alumni" to make a career in railroading include Chris Rohde, a Union Pacific engineer, and Bill Stetler, current head of the Canadian Pacific Railway's steam program. (Courtesy Phil Reader.)

Whether painting structures, pruning hedges, or restoring the railroad's passenger cars, the Wildcat Railroad could always depend on Al Martin. A World War II veteran, Martin was a multifaceted volunteer with unparalleled devotion. The groundskeeper and "roustabout" on the Wildcat for more than two decades, his final project was the restoration of the railroad's entire passenger car fleet to its current, pristine state. (Courtesy Phil Reader.)

Five

THE HEISLER *ELK*

Along with friends Charlie Ward, Neil Vodden, Richard Lucas, and Charlie Givens, brothers Jim and Dick Holmes purchased a two-truck, narrow-gauge Heisler locomotive in 1955 at Prather Mill, California. Regulars at Billy Jones's ranch, they wanted to build a small-scale railroad of their own. Jim Holmes leans against the steam chest of his new acquisition while brother Dick looks on from the cab. The locomotive, dubbed the *Elk* by Charlie Ward, was soon moved to Billy Jones's prune orchard for restoration. (Courtesy Tom Shreve; Charlie Ward collection.)

The future *Elk* lies abandoned in the snow in January 1955. Built in 1911 for the Richardson Lumber Company of Stewart's Point, California, the 18-ton Heisler arrived in Lake County in the early 1920s, ending its career three decades later under the Prather Box Company. (Courtesy Tom Shreve; Charlie Ward collection.)

Neil Vodden expresses his disdain for a railfan camera while Jim Holmes, seen beside the rear truck, works to get the Heisler upright. One of three major types of geared locomotives, a Heisler uses two cylinders mounted inward on the frame in a "V" shape, powering a center driveshaft that transfers power to two or more trucks. Designed to handle sharp curves and steep grades, Heislers were ideally suited for logging and other industrial operations. (Courtesy Tom Shreve; Charlie Ward collection.)

Getting the Heisler to Los Gatos was no easy task. After forgetting to oil the center pins, the first attempt to load the locomotive failed. The movement was further complicated when clearance issues required the crew to shovel out hillsides to allow passage. While the load was no problem on the Golden Gate Bridge, the stability of this sagging span was questionable. (Courtesy Jim Holmes.)

Wedged between foliage, the *Elk* is carefully backed into Billy Jones's orchard. Steam-powered commutes could still be seen running into town when this photograph was taken, though the rails would be gone altogether when the little Heisler left the property in 1959. (Courtesy Jim Holmes.)

Neil Vodden steam cleans years of accumulated grease and rust from the *Elk* using the boiler of Billy Jones's 2-Spot as a stationary source of steam. A small, vertical boiler was later acquired to perform this task. (Courtesy Jim Holmes.)

Neil Vodden, pictured at left, and Jim Holmes stand beside the *Elk*'s original cab before its disposal. Despite the objections of Billy Jones, who insisted only a steel cab would be appropriate for a Heisler, a wooden replacement was fashioned in Neil Vodden's University Avenue basement. (Courtesy Jim Holmes.)

In 1956, the Elk's restoration begins to take shape. Although the locomotive was sold in 1959, the headlight, originating from the Bay Point and Clayton Railroad, remained with Charlie Ward. In 1962, he placed it on Roaring Camp and Big Trees No. 1, the *Dixiana*, where, despite brief absences over the years, it has remained ever since. (Courtesy Jim Holmes.)

The *Elk* restoration crew and friends pose with their small stationary boiler. Pictured, from left to right, are Junior "Gene" O'Lague, an SP hogger who still runs on the Santa Cruz, Big Trees and Pacific Railroad; Richard Lucas, a Sierra Railroad steam engineer; Dick Holmes (seen feeding the injector); Charlie Givens; and Jim Holmes, an SP signalman. (Photograph by Charlie Ward; courtesy Tom Shreve.)

For the first time in over a decade, the beast has returned to life. Though far from finished, the *Elk* was mechanically complete enough to justify being fired up for a steam test in this 1956 view. (Courtesy Jim Holmes.)

Dick Holmes and Richard Lucas, a Sierra Railroad steam engineer, bend the exhaust for the turbogenerator (dynamo). Jim Holmes's exquisite wooden pilot inspired Billy Jones to attempt his own woodworking project, resulting in the creation of the Wildcat's caboose from an Overfair flatcar. (Courtesy Jim Holmes.)

Running back and forth on a short and extremely light stretch of panel track, the *Elk* is nearly complete in this 1957 view. After the accidental disposition of the original stack, an oversized replacement, formerly atop a Caspar Lumber Company Mallet, took its place on the petite Heisler. (Courtesy Jim Holmes.)

Part of the *Elk* restoration crew shows off its work to Wildcat Railroad visitors. Pictured, from left to right, are John Carrick, Charlie Givens, and Peter Hahn. While retaining its original lap-seam boiler, the *Elk* possesses the later I-beam frame (versus the split-frame design seen on earlier Heislers). A menagerie of whistles, including a Southern Pacific short-bell five chime (or "Desert Chime"), enabled the crew to have some fun. (Courtesy Jim Holmes.)

More than a year after steam was retired on the Southern Pacific, the *Elk* was hot and running in 1958, giving it the distinction of being the last full-scale steam locomotive to operate in Los Gatos. An original Overfair Railway boxcar is seen at left, sitting on rails no lighter than those the 18-ton Heisler is running on. (Courtesy Jim Holmes.)

Shortly after its completion, the *Elk* was sold to the late Harold "Hal" Wilmunder of Roseville. An avid collector of narrow-gauge equipment, Wilmunder operated the engine on his backyard Antelope and Western Railroad until establishing the Camino, Cable and Northern tourist operation in 1967. Spending years in storage, the locomotive was a static display at the California State Railroad Museum's Railfair '81. It is currently undergoing restoration in Butte County. (Courtesy Jim Holmes.)

Six

THE FINAL COMMUTE

For more than eight decades, the railroad was a lifeline to Los Gatos. While the route to Santa Cruz was severed in 1940, steam and later diesel-powered commutes would continue to serve Los Gatos until January 1959, when the two-and-a-half-mile branch into downtown was removed. In this c. 1950 view, P-6 Pacific No. 2458 runs around her train after arriving from San Francisco. It will deadhead tender first to San Jose for the night and return tender first the next morning. (Photograph by Charlie Givens; courtesy Eddie Chase.)

In this *c.* 1955 view, No. 2477, a 4-6-2, brings the southbound commute into Los Gatos Depot, a 1924 remodel of the original 1878 South Pacific Coast structure. A Class P-7 built by the Lima Locomotive Works for the Arizona Eastern Railway, 2477, along with sister 2476, were the mainstay of steam-commute power into Los Gatos during its final years of operation. (Photograph by Charlie Givens; courtesy Eddie Chase.)

After a hard day's work and an hour-and-a-half train ride, commuters head for their automobiles and drive home. This early 1950s photograph at Los Gatos Depot truly "freeze frames" the era of commute service into Los Gatos. The depot area is now occupied by Town Plaza, the freight shed's location is marked by the present post office, and Montebello Way, the street running parallel to the depot, is now substantially narrower. (Courtesy Charlie Givens.)

Train No. 132, the southbound, weekday commute, has just passed Vasona Junction, continuing on the final two-and-a-half-mile leg of its journey from San Francisco. This grassy knoll, a frequent location for railfan photographs, has since been leveled and is now occupied by an office park at Lark and University Avenues. (Courtesy Eddie Chase.)

Engine No. 2402, an early P-4 class Pacific, steams above Vasona Reservoir on its deadhead journey back to San Jose. This portion of right-of-way became an extended University Avenue in the early 1960s. (Courtesy Los Gatos Public Library.)

Steaming through a pair of ancient semaphores, Train No. 132 approaches Williams Street (Blossom Hill Road) Crossing. In 1955, a new town park was established at Oak Meadow, formerly the town sewer farm, after the Highway 17 bypass displaced the original park located beneath the Main Street Bridge. The ancestral oaks that line the perimeter of Oak Meadow can be seen in the background of this *c.* 1955 view, which depicts engine 2477 in what is now the AAA parking lot. (Courtesy Jim Holmes.)

The brakeman rides the point as No. 2477 couples pilot first onto her train. Crider's Department Store, beneath its 1940s facade, is former depot agent Eugene Ford's 1904 Opera House. Note the train number boards have already been changed to designate the deadhead movement back to San Jose. (Courtesy Jim Holmes.)

88

Lima-built No. 2477 crosses Main Street–guarded by an early wigwag crossing signal–as it runs around its train c. 1955. The Novitiate Winery, an active freight client at the time, can be seen atop the hill in the background. This lighter Pacific was later fitted with a larger, six-axle tender during its final days of operation. (Courtesy Jim Holmes.)

Parking already occupies a portion of the former Los Gatos yard as a deadheading No. 2477 crosses Elm Street around 1955. The "Free Parking" sign marks the approximate location of the turntable and adjacent enginehouse, which stood in Los Gatos until about 1918. Note the pilot on the tender of No. 2477, which made the nine-mile reverse trip to San Jose regularly. (Courtesy Jim Holmes.)

Train No. 129, the weekday morning commute, steams above Vasona Reservoir after its 6:40 a.m. departure from Los Gatos. The northbound train will make about a dozen stops before dashing at mainline speed to San Francisco's Third and Townsend passenger terminal. As the morning train pulled into Los Gatos, it is said the melodic six-chime whistles would echo three times off the mountains, an effective wake-up call for the entire town. (Photograph by Charlie Ward; courtesy Tom Shreve.)

While the details of this photograph are unknown, it appears to feature a morning commute, headed by No. 2476, possibly crossing a recently paved Lark Avenue. Today a four-lane road, Lark Avenue graduated from dustbowl status only a few years prior to the railroad's removal. (Courtesy Jim Holmes.)

Engine 2476 poses at an unknown location, perhaps at the beginning of the San Jose–Campbell–Vasona line at Sunol and San Carlos Streets in San Jose. Train No. 132, however, was the weekday evening commute, which would more likely place this photograph north of Los Gatos, possibly near California Avenue. (Courtesy Jim Holmes.)

With the weekday morning commute in tow, No. 2476 steams up the northern portion of the Mayfield Cut-Off at Neal, near Palo Alto. After diverging from the Peninsula mainline, the branch skirted Stanford University and the present-day Gunn High School football field before continuing south in the future footprint of Foothill Expressway. While the highway accounts for the majority of lost right-of-way, the portion from California Avenue to Alta Mesa, north of Arastradero Road, remains traceable today. It was used as an industrial spur until 1982. (Courtesy Jim Holmes.)

A Saturday afternoon commute approaches Royce Street Crossing in downtown Los Gatos. Discontinued in 1953, this train reflects an era when the average workweek lasted five and a half days. As with the rest of the old right-of-way between Main Street and Los Gatos-Saratoga Road, this portion of the line is now parking. (Courtesy Eddie Chase.)

Leading a Central Coast Railway Club special, No. 2476 nears Williams Street Crossing on April 25, 1954. Patrons enjoyed a ride on Billy Jones's Wildcat Railroad along with a rare photograph opportunity as the train backed to Los Gatos. Industrial Way, the narrow street parallel to University and North Santa Cruz Avenues, occupies the former right-of-way from this point to Los Gatos-Saratoga Road. (Courtesy Jim Holmes.)

4-6-2 No. 2458 poses beside the 1878 South Pacific Coast freight shed after hauling the evening weekday commute, Train No. 132, into Los Gatos. A 1913 product of ALCO's Brooks Works, No. 2458 and her sisters, typically assigned to the San Francisco-Pacific Grove *Del Monte*, were fitted with unusually short tenders to fit onto the small turntable at Pacific Grove. The blaring of an air horn would announce the P-6's occasional appearances in Los Gatos, though a melodious SP six chime would accompany their exit in reverse. No. 2458 was sold to a Los Angeles junker in 1955 but resurfaced in stationary boiler service at Calexico, California, in 1959. (Photograph by Charlie Givens; courtesy Eddie Chase.)

In this *c.* 1953 view, No. 2477, running tender first, drags an empty train back to San Jose. Built by Pullman beginning in 1923, the Southern Pacific's distinctive 72-foot suburban commute coaches, or "Subs," would remain in use on the Peninsula until 1985 when new CalTrain equipment arrived. (Photograph by Charlie Givens; courtesy Eddie Chase.)

A sign of changing times, the Saturday afternoon commute was discontinued after April 25, 1953. Engine No. 2477 did the honors, leading Train No. 168 into town one last time. (Photograph by Charlie Givens; courtesy Eddie Chase.)

Engine No. 2477 runs around Train No. 168 for the last time. Pictured at left is the town garden, which added a pleasing aesthetic element in contrast to the overgrown tracks. The observation car was chartered by local railroad enthusiasts. (Courtesy Eddie Chase.)

The engineer changes the train number boards to designate the deadhead movement to San Jose. A captivated young audience looks on from the observation car as Nos. 1, 6, and 8 are removed for the last time. (Courtesy Eddie Chase.)

Two young Los Gatans witness the departure of Engine No. 2477. With the days of steam numbered, these boys were privileged to have witnessed the most glorious chapter in railroading history. (Courtesy Eddie Chase.)

The conductor gazes curiously at the camera while the engineer descends from the locomotive. The number assigned to the Saturday afternoon deadhead was 191. (Courtesy Eddie Chase.)

Engines No. 2476 and No. 2477, both Lima-built Class P-7s, pose at San Francisco's Mission Bay roundhouse, home base for the Southern Pacific's passenger fleet. The two Arizona Eastern veterans, seen during the final months of their careers, were the regular power for the Los Gatos commutes during the final years of steam. (Photograph by Stan Kistler; courtesy Eddie Chase.)

Steam Engines Retired

OLD LOCOMOTIVE GOES—Another step in modernizing Los Gatos Southern Pacific passenger service was taken Friday when the local train first arrived in town powered by a diesel-electric locomotive. The two The above shot, near Saratoga avenue, was made just before the semaphore signal with the blade was replaced, and while the line was still steam-powered. Most commute trains on the peninsula service are dieselized.

In January 1957, the steam locomotive would disappear from the Los Gatos commute and the rest of the Southern Pacific system, months after dieselization of the line's freight service. A Fairbanks-Morse H-24-66 "Train Master" became the first diesel locomotive to handle the run, though displaced shortly thereafter by newer SD7 and SD9 units. The arrival of the "dieasel" was preceded by the October 1 installation of modern "searchlight" signals, replacing the semaphores that stood guard in Los Gatos for more than a half century. (Courtesy Eddie Chase.)

SD7 No. 5339 crosses Main Street as it brings the evening commute into town. The units of choice on the Los Gatos run, SDs were not the only diesels to shine an "ashcan" headlight over Los Gatos. In 1957, a raging fire erupted at a box factory near San Jose's Cahill Street station. As hoses lay across the rails, dispatchers rerouted the northbound Coast Daylight through Vasona Junction and up the Mayfield Cut-Off. Pushed by a Fairbanks-Morse switch engine, diners on the tail end enjoyed views of Vasona Reservoir as the lengthy train cleared the wye to continue forward. The Daylight may have been late to San Francisco that evening, but the SP's most celebrated mainline passenger train had humbly passed through Los Gatos. (Photograph by E. H. Chase; courtesy Eddie Chase.)

In stark contrast to the ornate wood-burners that first served this line, SD9 No. 5362 leads a train of modern, double-deck Gallery cars in this c. 1958 view. Similar to the cars currently in use on CalTrain, Gallery cars were typically featured on evening commutes while the older "Subs" made up morning trains. (Courtesy Mary Gillespie-Greenberg.)

This April 25, 1954, view juxtaposes the previous photograph with one from the days of steam. No. 2476 is on the point of the Central Coast Railway Club excursion. Steam locomotives had their obvious share of problems but were reliable machines in comparison to "first generation" diesels. In September 1958, a Train Master unit on the Los Gatos commute stalled a short distance from the depot. An ALCO switcher pulled the disabled locomotive and its empty train of Gallery cars through downtown Los Gatos. The incident repeated with SD7 No. 5330 in the spring of 1957. (Courtesy Jim Holmes.)

On June 2, 1957, to commemorate the retirement of Southern Pacific's general passenger agent, T. Louis Chess, a steam locomotive, was brought into Los Gatos one last time. Originating in San Francisco, the special traveled down the Mayfield Cut-Off to Vasona, and then backed to the Los Gatos Depot. On the return trip, the train stopped at Farley Road, where passengers walked to a celebration hosted at Billy Jones's ranch and railroad. (Photograph by E. H. Chase; courtesy Eddie Chase.)

Railroad enthusiasts crowd the observation deck of the *El Dorado*, chartered by the Central Coast Railway Club, as the T. Louis Chess Retirement Special backs towards Los Gatos. Chess helped organize many excursions during his tenure as general passenger agent. The Gallery car double-deck commute, visible at right, had the dubious distinction of being the first of its type run into Los Gatos. (Photograph by E. H. Chase; courtesy Eddie Chase.)

Built by Cooke in 1896, 4-6-0 No. 2248 was among the last and oldest steam locomotives to see service on the Southern Pacific. After years on the Donner Pass fire train, the Southern Pacific "backdated" the ten-wheeler in 1955 to participate in special events. In the photograph at left, No. 2248 poses near the Standard Oil facility on Farley Road. (Photograph by E. H. Chase; courtesy Eddie Chase.)

Passengers on the T. Louis Chess Retirement Special detrain at Farley Road, where they will walk a short distance to enjoy a barbeque and train ride at Billy Jones's ranch. Engine No. 2248 remains operable today as the *Tarantula Train* on Texas's Grapevine Vintage Railroad. (Photograph by E. H. Chase; courtesy Eddie Chase.)

In the mid-1950s, the Southern Pacific investigated abandoning the two-and-a-half-mile "stub" from Vasona Junction to downtown. By relocating the commuter stop to Vasona, the runaround procedure could be eliminated. On January 23, 1959 at 7:59 p.m., engineer L. H. Cleveland highballed the last scheduled commute train back to San Jose, ending 81 years of passenger service into town. The following morning, the Central Coast Railway Club sponsored a "Pulling of the Spike" ceremony along with a final excursion to San Jose. More than 1,200 spectators showed up to bid farewell to Los Gatos's railroad. (Courtesy Jones family.)

"Honorary Engineer" Billy Jones strikes a pose while the Los Gatos High School pep band plays a dirge from Engine No. 5624. After a first train ran to San Jose and returned, chamber of commerce vice president Bert Holmes addressed the crowd with these remarks, "It was customary to drive the last spike when a railroad is completed, but now with the railroad leaving Los Gatos, we'll pull the spikes." A lighthearted Jones added, "Los Gatos will still have a railroad; you can ride mine anytime." (Courtesy Jones family.)

Dressed in their best, Los Gatans pay their final respects at this requiem for the railroad in this uniquely overexposed view. While reportedly only 12 commuters remained from the downtown depot, the turnout during the January 24 ceremony further proved the railroad's importance to a Los Gatos of days gone by. Tickets for the absolute last trip quickly sold out, though additional cars added at San Jose allowed 1,255 passengers to sardine into the double-deck coaches. (Courtesy Jones family.)

There was silence as R. A. Miller, Coast Division superintendent, pulled the first spike and presented it to Los Gatos mayor Alberto Merrill. Following the ceremony, the train made its final run to San Jose, returning not to the downtown depot but to the new stop at Vasona Junction. Engine No. 5624, a "Torpedo Boat" GP9 (so named for its long, hood-mounted air tanks), remained in Peninsula commute service well into the 1980s. Renumbered 3195, the former No. 5624 was scrapped at Richmond in 1993. Its rear pilot survives on sister No. 5623, restored and operated by owners Errol Ohman and Howard Wise on the Niles Canyon Railway. (Courtesy Eddie Chase.)

This rare, c. 1964 photograph shows a forlorn Los Gatos Depot following the removal of the railroad it had been built to serve. Railway Express Agency continued to operate out of the south end of the building until 1961. (Courtesy *Los Gatos Weekly-Times*; John Baggerly collection.)

Sporting the experimental Halloween paint scheme, GP9 No. 5601 leads a southbound commute past Vasona Junction in 1960, one year after the track into town was removed. In 1963, with 170 commuters remaining between Vasona and Mayfield, the Interstate Commerce Commission denied the Southern Pacific's initial request to abandon West Valley commute service. By January 1964, the SP succeeded in their petition to the ICC ruling, resulting in the removal of the 6.2 miles between Simla and Alta Mesa. Vasona Wye, which remained intact until this time, was also severed, leaving only the north leg for approach by the Permanente Local. (Courtesy Eddie Chase.)

By the end of 1964, the nearly 90-year-old depot became the latest "postcard landmark" in Los Gatos to meet the wrecking ball. Its razing came approximately two years after that of the Hotel Lyndon, which neighbored the railroad for the better part of a century. (Courtesy *Los Gatos Weekly-Times*; John Baggerly collection.)

Seven

ON TO OAK MEADOW

Billy Jones was gone, but thanks to overwhelming community effort, his railroad lived on. In March 1968, the Los Gatos Jaycees offered to purchase the 2-Spot and passenger cars if the town provided both a place for operations and a small subsidy for maintenance costs. Interested, the town began investigation of the proposal. This sketch of the proposed Oak Meadow Depot was rendered by artist Marvin Bamburg. (Courtesy Phil Reader.)

While local businessman Bill Mason organized a committee to raise the needed funds to purchase the railroad, the Jones heirs, who wanted the railroad to remain in town, turned down generous offers from commercial developers. To encourage donations to the cause, the Wildcat's caboose was placed on display at Old Town shopping center. Eventually the decision was made to relocate the line to Oak Meadow and neighboring Vasona parks. This photograph shows two young volunteers removing ties on the weekend of March 29, 1969. (Courtesy Barbara Phinney; BJWRR collection.)

The people and businesses of Los Gatos and the rest of Santa Clara Valley extended a helping hand to save the Wildcat Railroad. Although the final fund-raising run at the ranch was held in July 1968, the 2-Spot, pictured here being loaded for its short trip to the park, was again under steam to assist in dismantling the line. (Courtesy Barbara Phinney; BJWRR collection.)

106

Over a single weekend, the Wildcat Railroad was moved from the Jones ranch to Oak Meadow Park. On March 29 and 30, 1969, volunteers swarmed both locations to load and unload the 2-Spot, four passenger cars, three freight cars, caboose, and stacks of rail and ties. Here a truckload containing three passenger coaches is ready to head down Daves Avenue. The original MacDermot-built cars were replaced by replicas in 1971. (Courtesy Barbara Phinney; BJWRR collection.)

Paul Morton, whose University Avenue machine shop often performed work for Billy Jones, poses with a loose and tired 2-Spot soon after its arrival at Oak Meadow Park. Completion of the new enginehouse, still months away, was far enough along to accept delivery of the 2-Spot and salvageable rolling stock. The enginehouse and depot were designed in the Carpenter's Gothic style by Higgins and Root of Los Gatos. (Courtesy Peter Panacy; BJWRR collection.)

While volunteers were hard at work building the new Wildcat Railroad, MacDermot Pacifics Nos. 1912 and 1913 remained in storage at Billy Jones's Daves Avenue ranch. With impending subdivision of the Jones property, Herb Ermert, Jones's son-in-law, proceeded to vacate the enginehouse by selling its two remaining occupants. Robert Maxfield, a Piedmont real estate developer, operated No. 1913 on his short-lived Calistoga Steam Railway from 1975 through 1979. In this November 1969 newspaper clipping, Maxfield poses with No. 1913 shortly before its departure from the Jones ranch. (Courtesy Los Gatos Public Library.)

The first rides on the new Billy Jones Wildcat Railroad were offered during the town's Fourth of July picnic in 1969. Still sporting Daylight colors, the tired teakettle ran back and forth on the 300 feet of track that had been laid. Short rides were again offered that September, when the Los Gatos Lions Club hosted their annual steak barbeque at the park. (Courtesy Barbara Phinney; BJWRR collection.)

Visitors admire the 2-Spot during one of the preliminary steam ups at the park in 1969. Bill Ulleseit, seen to the immediate left of the locomotive, was a lead volunteer in the complete overhaul of the locomotive in the months that followed. (Courtesy Barbara Phinney; BJWRR collection.)

Volunteers construct the original 25-foot turntable at Oak Meadow Park, used from 1970 to 1996. The Seabees, a U.S. Navy construction battalion, assisted in its creation, and Bill Mason and his wife, Kamille, often prepared lunch for laborers. The cooks, or "Lizard Scorchers" in railroad terminology, once triggered a false alarm for the local fire department, whose hoses rained down on Mason's smoked salmon lunch. (Courtesy Barbara Phinney; BJWRR collection.)

A Southern Pacific piggyback flatcar is lifted into place over Los Gatos Creek, where it will serve as the first of the BJWRR's two bridges. Wrecked on the mainline, the 89-foot car body was acquired from a Solano County dealer and has been used to span the creek ever since. (Courtesy Barbara Phinney; BJWRR collection.)

Exhausted after 25 years at the Jones ranch, the 2-Spot was in need of a complete rebuild. Local machine shops permitted volunteers, such as master machinists Severn Edmonds and Bill Ulleseit, to use their facilities to work on parts of the locomotive. In this early 1970 view, reassembly of the running gear is well underway. Bill Ulleseit poses beside his work. (Courtesy Barbara Phinney; BJWRR collection.)

Sitting on stacks of ties, the 2-Spot's original boiler waits to be reunited with the restored running gear. (Courtesy Barbara Phinney; BJWRR collection.)

On July 26, 1970, the new Billy Jones Wildcat Railroad began operation on the initial loop around Squirrel Hill. Since that time, the railroad, now approximately a mile long, has attracted over a million riders. In 1973, it gained national exposure as a featured segment on Charles Kuralt's *On the Road* television program. In the above view, a restored 2-spot poses for a formal portrait near the Los Gatos Creek Trail crossing. (Courtesy Barbara Phinney; BJWRR collection.)

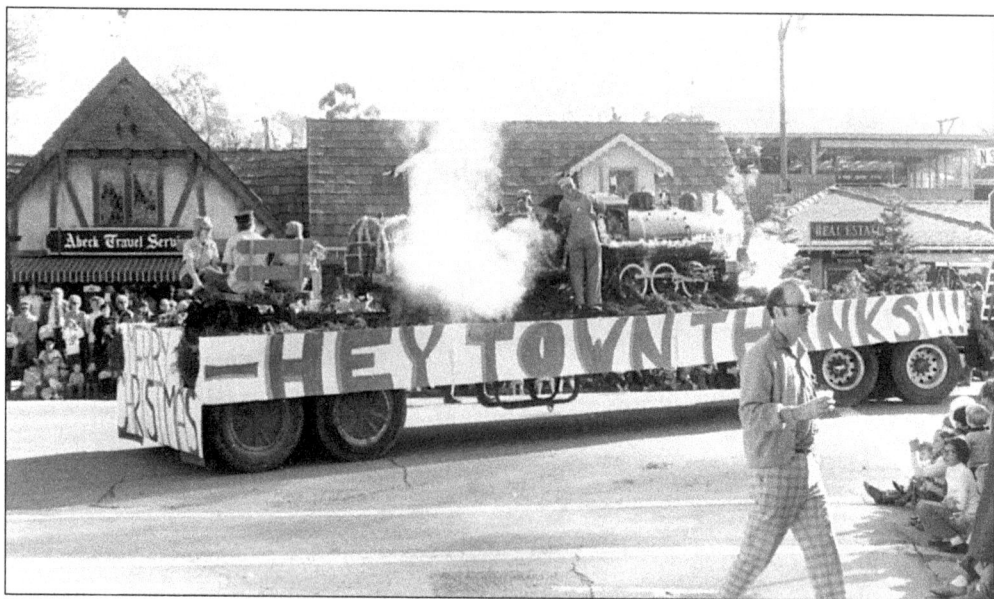

Few floats in the Children's Holiday Parade can boast a locomotive, but the 2-Spot is hot and under steam as it rolls past the Little Village Shops on North Santa Cruz Avenue in 1970. A banner proclaiming, "Hey Town, Thanks!," expresses gratitude to loyal members of the community who pulled together to help establish the railroad at Oak Meadow Park. (Courtesy Barbara Phinney; BJWRR collection.)

In 1973, 18-year-old Dorothy Beattie became the Wildcat Railroad's first female engineer. "I'm not for women's lib," she commented in a *Los Gatos Times-Observer* interview. "I just wanted to run the train." The Wildcat has since produced about a half-dozen other female engineers, a number that will hopefully continue to increase in the future. (Courtesy Barbara Phinney; BJWRR collection.)

Rumors speculating the whereabouts and survival of the 2-Spot's older sibling, Eastlake Park Railway No. 1903, were of great interest to BJWRR president Bill Mason, who had hopes of acquiring it as a second locomotive. A successful search ended at a Scio, Oregon, farm where owner Bill Krauss had little use for the 18-inch locomotive on his two-foot gauge railroad. The locomotive was placed on long-term lease in 1972 and sold outright to the railroad 20 years later. (Courtesy Barbara Phinney; BJWRR collection.)

No. 1903 was placed into service at Los Angeles's Eastlake Park in 1901. The prototype for the improved Venice Railway locomotives, John Coit kept the stout 2-6-0 as the backup engine at Venice for several years. Briefly operated in San Bernardino, it was sold to an Oregon amusement park by 1920, after which point it went rogue for nearly 50 years. When the locomotive was discovered in a field, a sheet-metal shell sat where the boiler once was, concealing the Ford Model A engine that had been installed to power it. A new boiler was built in the 1970s and it is hoped the locomotive will again operate under steam as BJWRR No. 3. (Courtesy Phil Reader.)

The railroad's original "Sylvester" logo, created in 1968 by board member Mike Kotowski, was somewhat controversial in its striking resemblance to the Looney Tunes character. After a Warner Brothers employee visited the railroad and hinted at the possibility of a lawsuit, the Sylvester mascot entered early retirement in favor of Kotowski's new "Billy Cat" herald. The questionable graphic was removed from circulation by the 1980s, but it remained on the railroad's handicapped-accessible coach for several years. (Courtesy Chuck Bergtold.)

BJWRR Master Mechanic Larry Ingold takes the 2-Spot for a run. The shiny stainless-steel boiler jacket was applied following a 1978 enginehouse fire, which destroyed the structure's cupola and sidelined the 2-Spot for six weeks. (Courtesy Barbara Phinney; BJWRR collection.)

In 1984, Homestake Gold Mine in South Dakota disposed of its fleet of 18-inch gauge compressed air locomotives in favor of newer equipment. As BJWRR was in the market for a second locomotive for maintenance of way service, managers Ken Middlebrook and Dave Johnson arranged the donation of Homestake No. 12, a five-ton H. K. Porter product of 1909. The two college students flew to Denver, where they rented a Hertz moving truck to transport the locomotive to Los Gatos. In the above photograph, Dave Johnson, left, witnesses the last movement of No. 12 on Homestake rails. (Photograph by Ken Middlebrook; courtesy Barbara Phinney.)

Bill Ulleseit, assisted by Bill Mason and others, carefully winches No. 12 off the truck after its arrival in Los Gatos. The five-ton locomotive was likely no strain for Mason, who was once offered a spot on the Green Bay Packers. (Photograph by Ken Middlebrook; courtesy Barbara Phinney.)

Using the railroad's wheelchair car as an idler, the No. 12, assisted by the 2-Spot, is rolled onto Wildcat rails for the first time. Compressed-air locomotives were intended for mining and industrial operations where exhaust fumes or sparks posed a problem. The locomotives' air reservoirs were charged by a stationary compressor, often to pressures exceeding 500 pounds per square inch, to provide lasting power for its 150-pound-per-square-inch pneumatic cylinders. (Photograph by Ken Middlebrook; courtesy Barbara Phinney.)

The Homestake No. 12 became somewhat of an unwanted stepchild at the BJWRR. As Billy Jones had experienced with his English quarry engine, the *Gwen*, the No. 12's wide flanges caused it to ride high over switch frogs. With the impending arrival of a new diesel locomotive, No. 12 was donated to the California State Railroad Museum in 1992. (Photograph by Ken Middlebrook; courtesy Barbara Phinney.)

A passenger waves excitedly while the 2-spot, with Phil Reader behind the throttle, runs across the trestle in Vasona Park. The 40-foot curved trestle, completed in 1972, was part of a 1,800-foot extension of the railroad, which resulted from requests for a longer ride. Its construction was made possible by the Saratoga Rotary Club, which donated lumber and other supplies, and civil engineer Brad Hunholt, who voluntarily performed the needed engineering work on the project. (Courtesy Phil Reader.)

George Barlow, chief engineer of England's 15-inch gauge Romney, Hythe and Dymchurch Railway, is given a cab ride by BJWRR engineer Phil Reader. (Courtesy Phil Reader.)

For several years, the 2-Spot participated under steam in the Los Gatos Children's Holiday Parade. Los Gatans could again hear the harmonic echo of a bronze, Southern Pacific six-chime whistle as the railroad's float cruised through town. (Courtesy Barbara Phinney; BJWRR collection.)

The 2-Spot rolls off the parade float back at Oak Meadow Park. Two floats were featured during the year Diesel No. 2502, visible in the background, was placed into service. Note the new water tower, built after the original fell victim to the 1989 earthquake. (Courtesy Barbara Phinney; BJWRR collection.)

Eight

STILL STEAMING ALONG

In 2005, after a decade-long absence, the echo of a steam locomotive whistle was again heard in Los Gatos. On July 24, the Billy Jones Wildcat Railroad celebrated the centennial and return of their beloved 2-Spot, which, needing a new boiler, was withdrawn from service in 1995. After 10 years and nearly 2,700 volunteer hours by Chief Engineer Bill Ulleseit, a fire was lit in the 2-Spot's new boiler for the first time. Longtime volunteer Ken Middlebrook had no problem showing up early to steam up the 2-Spot. He takes a break while his wife, Katie, also a qualified steam engineer, gets some throttle time in February 2006. (Courtesy author.)

The Wildcat Railroad's first step towards modernization came with the delivery of its first diesel locomotive in 1992. Based on EMD's modern GP-60M, No. 2502 was built by Custom Locomotive Works of Chicago using a design supplied by volunteers Randy Jones and Ken Reiter. Painted in the Southern Pacific "black widow" scheme, the locomotive proudly carries the name *Albert B. Smith* in honor of the man who made its construction possible. (Courtesy *Los Gatos Weekly-Times*.)

Bill Ulleseit and Katie Middlebrook inspect the 2-Spot before a day's run. (Courtesy *Los Gatos Weekly-Times*.)

After 91 years, with the majority of that time spent in regular service, the 2-Spot's original boiler reached the end of its service life. Volunteer Al Martin looks on as it is lifted off the running gear. (Courtesy Barbara Phinney; BJWRR collection.)

From 1995 to 2005, Diesel No. 2502 was the railroad's sole operating motive power. Subject to constant use, with downtime not an option, the locomotive took heavy abuse. A new Isuzu diesel engine was purchased, but given the locomotive could not be out of service to have it installed, it remained crated. Desperate, the order for a second diesel locomotive was placed with Custom Locomotive Works in 2001. After that company went bankrupt, the job was transferred to Merrick Light Railway Equipment Works of Wisconsin. No. 3502 is pictured here beside No. 2502 shortly after its delivery in December 2005. (Courtesy author.)

Due to the Wildcat Railroad's unusual layout, it is necessary to turn the locomotive and run it around its train after every run. The location of the original 1970 turntable was problematic with longer trains because, while sitting in the station, the locomotive would effectively block the busy crossing. To rectify this decades-old problem, the decision was made to construct a new turntable further down the line. With Ken and Katie Middlebrook "in the cab," the 2-Spot gets a spin on the new turntable in February 2006. (Courtesy author.)

Engineer Ken Middlebrook greases a crankpin while the 2-spot is topped off with fuel and water. As with a number of steam-operating railroads today, the Wildcat Railroad has adopted No. 2 diesel, a cleaner-burning alternative to heavier oils, as its fuel of choice. Burning No. 2 is also advantageous in that only a single facility is required to fuel both steam and diesel locomotives. (Courtesy author.)

Billy Jones once chuckled when a young Al Smith spoke of his dreams to someday own the Overfair Railway Pacifics. In 1978, Smith purchased Engine No. 1912 and No. 1913 from Bob Maxfield and began construction of his two-and-a-half-mile Swanton Pacific Lines the following year. After the death of Quentin Jervis, the last surviving member of Overfair Corporation, Smith acquired Nos. 1914 and 1915 at a 1983 auction. The winning bid for No. 1500 was from none other than Neil Vodden, who would keep his locomotive at Swanton. Nos. 1912 and 1914 are seen under steam during the Swanton Pacific's annual Al Smith Day runs on April 9, 2006. (Courtesy author.)

Built by Louis MacDermot, saved by Billy Jones, nearly sold to Disney, and scattered across California for two decades, Al Smith reunited and established a permanent home for the long-nomadic Overfair Railway equipment. Smith left his 3,200-acre Swanton Pacific Ranch and its railroad to Cal Poly, his alma mater, and the nonprofit Swanton Pacific Railroad Society continues to operate, maintain, and improve the railroad today. Nos. 1912 and 1914 are pictured here during Al Smith Day 2006. Engine No. 1913 and No. 1500 are currently under restoration at Swanton, while the never-completed 1915 was donated to the California State Railroad Museum. (Photograph by Brenden Neumayr.)

BJWRR executive director Peter Panacy takes the 2-Spot for a run in January 2006. The unusually warm winter weather brought out enough passengers to justify a four-car train. (Courtesy author.)

Despite the abandonment of West Valley commute service by 1964, the tracks would remain in place through Vasona, pictured here c. 2005. Along with the San Jose–Campbell–Vasona line and the Kaiser Cement Corporation's 1.7-mile spur, the more than seven remaining miles of the original Mayfield Cut-Off became the Southern Pacific's Vasona Branch. The north leg of the wye is all that remains of the former junction, pictured here around 2005. Courtside Club's parking lot now occupies the site of the southern leg. (Courtesy author.)

A train of empties from the Hanson-Permanente Cement Plant rolls across the Wedgewood Avenue crossing in 2005. Union Pacific, Southern Pacific's successor in 1996, has downgraded the branch to industrial lead status, though it continues to make significant upgrades and improvements. The Permanente Local, which supplies coal for the Cupertino plant's kilns, typically warrants the power of multiple locomotives to make the steep grade north of Monta Vista. (Courtesy author.)

A 1980s movement spearheaded by Santa Clara County supervisor Rod Diridon engulfed San Jose in a trolley renaissance. Nearly a half-century since its initial demise, trolley service returned in the form of a modern light rail system, one which now operates more than 50 miles of service throughout the Santa Clara Valley. In 2000, the dream of establishing light rail service to Los Gatos came closer to reality when the Valley Transportation Authority purchased the six-mile right-of-way from San Jose to Vasona Junction. Phase one of the Vasona Light Rail corridor was completed in October 2005, inaugurating service to Winchester Station in Campbell. A final phase will extend the terminus to the north side of Highway 85, the border of Los Gatos. (Courtesy author.)

Could a modern commute train to Santa Cruz alleviate congestion over Highway 17? Beginning in 1988, the Eccles and Eastern laid the groundwork to reconstruct the old mountain line between Vasona Junction and Olympia, the end of track on the Santa Cruz, Big Trees and Pacific Railroad north of Felton. The privately held company, which had hopes of running both freight and passenger service along with a steam excursion train, determined the 16-mile gap could be rebuilt with only four miles of realignment around Los Gatos. A bypass could be built around Lexington Reservoir, while the center of Highway 17 offered a more practical route around downtown with minimal noise pollution. Despite a strong following, the Eccles and Eastern abandoned their efforts after opposition by mountain residents and reorganized as the Sierra Pacific Coast Railway in 1995. (Author's collection.)

Overgrown and forgotten, these two original rails lie in the weeds beside the downtown Highway 17 on-ramp, a humble and unintentional tribute to the railroads of Los Gatos. Unless a rail transit-embracing future lies ahead, these two sticks of steel may be the last downtown Los Gatos will ever see of the railroad. (Courtesy author.)

126

Nearly 130 years since the first steam train rolled into town, Los Gatos continues to enjoy its last railroad. With the 2005 return of the 2-Spot, the Billy Jones Wildcat Railroad once again provides a place for Los Gatans to experience a real steam locomotive. While the nonprofit corporation provides paying jobs to high-school and college students, devoted volunteers form the backbone of the little railroad, running the 2-Spot on weekends and performing needed maintenance on workdays. The aura and mystique that surrounds the lost Santa Cruz Mountain rail line will continue to enthrall all who learn about it, but thanks to a great engineer's legacy and the countless individuals who help keep it alive, the railroading spirit lives on in Los Gatos. (Courtesy Phil Reader.)

Visit us at
arcadiapublishing.com

www.ingramcontent.com/pod-product-compliance
Lightning Source LLC
Chambersburg PA
CBHW050542110426
42813CB00008B/2237